Surface Computing and Collaborative Analysis Work

Synthesis Lectures on Human-Centered Informatics

Editor
John M. Carroll, *Penn State University*

Human-Centered Informatics (HCI) is the intersection of the cultural, the social, the cognitive, and the aesthetic with computing and information technology. It encompasses a huge range of issues, theories, technologies, designs, tools, environments and human experiences in knowledge work, recreation and leisure activity, teaching and learning, and the potpourri of everyday life. The series will publish state-of-the-art syntheses, case studies, and tutorials in key areas. It will share the focus of leading international conferences in HCI.

Geographical Design: Spatial Cognition and Geographical Information Science
Stephen C. Hirtle
2011

User-Centered Agile Methods
Hugh Beyer
2010

Experience-Centered Design: Designers, Users, and Communities in Dialogue
Peter Wright and John McCarthy
2010

Experience Design: Technology for All the Right Reasons
Marc Hassenzahl
2010

Designing and Evaluating Usable Technology in Industrial Research: Three Case Studies
Clare-Marie Karat and John Karat
2010

Interacting with Information
Ann Blandford and Simon Attfield
2010

Designing for User Engagement: Aesthetic and Attractive User Interfaces
Alistair Sutcliffe
2009

Context-Aware Mobile Computing: Affordances of Space, Social Awareness, and Social Influence
Geri Gay
2009

Studies of Work and the Workplace in HCI: Concepts and Techniques
Graham Button and Wes Sharrock
2009

Semiotic Engineering Methods for Scientific Research in HCI
Clarisse Sieckenius de Souza and Carla Faria Leitão
2009

Common Ground in Electronically Mediated Conversation
Andrew Monk
2008

Surface Computing and Collaborative Analysis Work

Judith Brown, Jeff Wilson, Stevenson Gossage, Chris Hack, and Robert Biddle

ISBN: 978-3-031-01074-3   paperback
ISBN: 978-3-031-02202-9   ebook

DOI 10.1007/978-3-031-02202-9

A Publication in the Springer series
SYNTHESIS LECTURES ON HUMAN-CENTERED INFORMATICS

Lecture #19
Series Editor: John M. Carroll, *Penn State University*
Series ISSN
Synthesis Lectures on Human-Centered Informatics
Print 1946-7680   Electronic 1946-7699

Surface Computing and Collaborative Analysis Work

Judith Brown, Jeff Wilson, Stevenson Gossage, Chris Hack, and Robert Biddle
Human-Oriented Technology Software Research Lab
Carleton University, Ottawa, Canada

SYNTHESIS LECTURES ON HUMAN-CENTERED INFORMATICS #19

ABSTRACT

Large surface computing devices (wall-mounted or tabletop) with touch interfaces and their application to collaborative data analysis, an increasingly important and prevalent activity, is the primary topic of this book. Our goals are to outline the fundamentals of surface computing (a still maturing technology), review relevant work on collaborative data analysis, describe frameworks for understanding collaborative processes, and provide a better understanding of the opportunities for research and development. We describe surfaces as display technologies with which people can interact directly, and emphasize how interaction design changes when designing for large surfaces. We review efforts to use large displays, surfaces or mixed display environments to enable collaborative analytic activity. Collaborative analysis is important in many domains, but to provide concrete examples and a specific focus, we frequently consider analysis work in the security domain, and in particular the challenges security personnel face in securing networks from attackers, and intelligence analysts encounter when analyzing intelligence data. Both of these activities are becoming increasingly collaborative endeavors, and there are huge opportunities for improving collaboration by leveraging surface computing. This work highlights for interaction designers and software developers the particular challenges and opportunities presented by interaction with surfaces. We have reviewed hundreds of recent research papers, and report on advancements in the fields of surface-enabled collaborative analytic work, interactive techniques for surface technologies, and useful theory that can provide direction to interaction design work. We also offer insight into issues that arise when developing applications for multi-touch surfaces derived from our own experiences creating collaborative applications. We present these insights at a level appropriate for all members of the software design and development team.

KEYWORDS

surface computing, interaction design, visualization, analysis, security analysis, collaboration, multi-touch frameworks

Contents

List of Figures

Acknowledgments

The authors wish to acknowledge support from NSERC, the Natural Sciences and Engineering Research Council of Canada, for funding through a Discovery Grant, and through SurfNet, the Strategic Research Network on Digital Surface Software Applications. We also wish to thank our research partners in industry, and especially Sharon Liff and Nadia Diakun-Thibault at the Government of Canada, for encouragement to begin this project and for their insightful comments and advice throughout the process. In addition, we are grateful to our anonymous referees for helpful comments and advice, and close colleagues, students and family members who provided feedback on drafts. Finally, we wish to thank Diane Cerra at Morgan & Claypool for her encouragement and help throughout the publication process.

Judith Brown, Jeff Wilson, Stevenson Gossage, Chris Hack, and Robert Biddle
August 2013

Figure Credits

Figure 2a	image used courtesy of SMART Technologies, `http://www.smarttech.com/`.
Figure 2b	image Copyright © 2013 Microsoft Corporation. Used with permission, `http://technet.microsoft.com/en-us/`.
Figure 2c	image Copyright © 1995-2013 SAMSUNG. All rights reserved. Used with permission, `http://www.samsung.com`.
Figure 4	image Copyright © 2009 ARTag. Used with permission, `http://www.artag.net/`.
Figures 5, 7	based on Isenberg, et al: Collaborative Visualization: Definition, Challenges, and Research Agenda. *Information Visualization Journal (IVS)*, 10(4): 310–326, 2011. Copyright © 2011 by SAGE Publications. Used with permission. DOI: 10.1177/1473871611412817
Figure 6	from Endert, et al: Professional analysts using a large, high- resolution display. In IEEE VAST 2009 (Extended Abstract) (Awarded Special Contributions to the VAST Challenge Contest), 2009. Copyright © 2009 IEEE. Used with permission.
Figures 8, 9	from Best, et al: Real-time visualization of network behaviors for situational awareness. *VizSec '10 Proceedings of the Seventh International Symposium on Visualization for Cyber Security*, pages 79-90, 2010. Copyright © 2010, Association for Computing Machinery, Inc. Reprinted by permission. DOI: 10.1145/1850795.1850805
Figure 10	from Wypych et al: System for inspection of large high-resolution radiography datasets. *Aerospace Conference, 2011 IEEE*. Copyright © 2011 IEEE. Used with permission. DOI: 10.1109/AERO.2011.5747534

Figure 11   from Browne, et al: Data analysis on interactive whiteboards through sketch-based interaction. *ITS '11 Proceedings of the ACM International Conference on Interactive Tabletops and Surfaces*, pages 154-157. Copyright © 2011, Association for Computing Machinery, Inc. Reprinted by permission. DOI: 10.1145/2076354.2076383

Figure 12   from Liu and Shi, uMeeting, an efficient co-located meeting system on the large-scale tabletop. In *Human-Computer Interaction. Users and Applications Lecture Notes in Computer Science*, Volume 6764, pages 368-374. Copyright © 2011, Springer Science+Business Media, LLC. Used with permission. DOI: 10.1007/978-3-642-21619-0_46

Figure 13   from Gumienny, et al: Tele-board: Enabling efficient collaboration in digital design spaces. *Proceedings of the 2011 15th International Conference on Computer Supported Cooperative Work in Design, CSCWD 2011, June 8-10, 2011, Lausanne, Switzerland*, pages 47-54. Copyright © 2011 IEEE. Used with permission. DOI: 10.1109/CSCWD.2011.5960054

Figures 14a, b   from Bradel, et al: *Space for two to think: Large, high-resolution displays for co-located collabo- rative sensemaking.* Technical Report TR-11-11, Computer Science, Virginia Tech, 2011. Used with permission.

Figure 15   from Isenberg, et al: An exploratory study of co-located collaborative visual analytics around a tabletop display. *Proceedings of IEEE VAST 2010*, pages 179–186. Copyright © 2011 IEEE. Used with permission.

Figures 16a, b   from Tobiasz, et al: Coordinating co-located collaboration with information visualization. *Visualization and Computer Graphics, IEEE Transactions on*, 15(6):1065–1072, Nov.-Dec. 2009. Copyright © 2009 IEEE. Used with permission. DOI: 10.1109/TVCG.2009.162

Figures 17a, b, c, d   from Tuddenham, et al: WebSurface: an interface for co-located collaborative information gathering. *ITS '09 Proceedings of the ACM International Conference on Interactive Tabletops and Surfaces*, pages 181–188. Copyright © 2009, Association for Computing Machinery, Inc. Reprinted by permission. DOI: 10.1145/1731903.1731938

Figure 18   from Browne, et al: Data analysis on interactive whiteboards through sketch-based interaction. *ITS '11 Proceedings of the ACM International Conference on Interactive Tabletops and Surfaces*, pages 154–157. Copyright © 2011, Association for Computing Machinery, Inc. Reprinted by permission. DOI: 10.1145/2076354.2076383

Figure 19   from Spindler, et al: Novel fields of application for tangible displays above the tabletop. *ITS '10 ACM International Conference on Interactive Tabletops and Surfaces*, pages 315–315. Copyright © 2010, Association for Computing Machinery, Inc. Reprinted by permission. DOI: 10.1145/1936652.1936743

Figures 20a, b   from Kirmizibayrak, et al: Evaluation of gesture based interfaces for medical volume visualization tasks. *VRCAI '11 Proceedings of the 10th International Conference on Virtual Reality Continuum and Its Applications in Industry*, pages 69–74. Copyright © 2011, Association for Computing Machinery, Inc. Reprinted by permission. DOI: 10.1145/2087756.2087764

Figure 21   from Dörk, et al: Visualizing explicit and implicit relations of complex information spaces. *Information Visualization Journal (IVS)*, 11:5–21, 2012. Copyright © 2012 by SAGE Publications. Used with permission. DOI: 10.1177/1473871611425872

Figure 22   from Wigdor, et al: WeSpace: The design development and deployment of a walk-up and share multi-surface visual collaboration system. *CHI '09 Proceedings of the SIGCHI Conference on Human Factors in Computing Systems*, pages 1237–1246. Copyright © 2009, Association for Computing Machinery, Inc. Reprinted by permission. DOI: 10.1145/1357054.1357266

Figure 23   from Song, et al: Wysiwyf: exploring and annotating volume data with a tangible handheld device. *CHI '11 Proceedings of the SIGCHI Conference on Human Factors in Computing Systems*, pages 1333–1342. Copyright © 2011, Association for Computing Machinery, Inc. Reprinted by permission. DOI: 10.1145/1978942.1979140

Figure 33a   from Mujibiya, et al: Anywhere touchtyping: text input on arbitrary surface using depth sensing. *UIST '10 Adjunct proceedings of the 23nd annual ACM symposium on User interface software and technology*, pages 443–444. Copyright © 2010, Association for Computing Machinery, Inc. Reprinted by permission. DOI: 10.1145/1866218.1866262

Figure 33b   from Murase, et al: Gesture keyboard requiring only one camera. *UIST '11 Adjunct: Proceedings of the 24th annual ACM symposium adjunct on User interface software and technology*, pages 9–10. Copyright © 2011, Association for Computing Machinery, Inc. Reprinted by permission. DOI: 10.1145/2046396.2046402

Figures 34a, b, c, d   from Schmidt, et al: IdLenses: dynamic personal areas on shared surfaces. *ITS '10 ACM International Conference on Interactive Table-tops and Surfaces*, pages 131–134. Copyright © 2010, Association for Computing Machinery, Inc. Reprinted by permission. DOI: 10.1145/1936652.1936678

Figures 35a, b, c, d, e, f   from Morris, et al: A field study of knowledge workers' use of interactive horizontal displays. *Horizontal Interactive Human Computer Systems, 2008. TABLETOP 2008. 3rd IEEE International Workshop on*, pages 105–112. Copyright © 2008 IEEE. Used with permission. DOI: 10.1109/TABLETOP.2008.4660192

Figure 36   from Czerwinski, et al: Toward characterizing the productivity benefits of very large displays. *Proceedings of INTERACT 2003*, pages 9–16. Copyright © 2003 IFIP. and from Robertson, et al: The large-display user experience," *IEEE Computer Graphics and Applications*, 25(4): 44–51, July-August 2005. Copyright © 2005 IEEE. Used with permission. DOI: 10.1109/MCG.2005.88

Figure 37   from Ball, et al: Analysis of user behavior on high-resolution tiled displays. *Human-Computer Interaction - INTERACT 2005: Proceedings of the IFIP TC13 International Conference, Rome, Italy, September 12-16, 2005*, pages 350–363. Copyright © 2005, Springer Science+Business Media, LLC. Used with permission. DOI: 10.1007/11555261_30

Figure 38   from Andrews, et al: Space to think: Large high-resolution displays for sensemaking. *CHI '10 Proceedings of the SIGCHI Conference on Human Factors in Computing Systems*, pages 55–64. Copyright © 2010, Association for Computing Machinery, Inc. Reprinted by permission. DOI: 10.1145/1753326.1753336

Figure 39 from Yost, et al: Beyond visual acuity: The perceptual scalability of information visualizations for large displays. *CHI '07 Proceedings of the SIGCHI Conference on Human Factors in Computing Systems*, pages 101–110. Copyright © 2007, Association for Computing Machinery, Inc. Reprinted by permission. DOI: 10.1145/1240624.1240639

Figure 40 from Riley, et al: Collaborative planning and situation awareness in army command and control. *Ergonomics*, 49(12-13):1139– 1153, 2006. Copyright © 2006 Taylor & Francis Group, LLC. Used with permission. DOI: 10.1080/00140130600612614

Figure 41 from Tuddenham and Robinson, Territorial coordination and workspace awareness in remote tabletop collaboration. *CHI '09 Proceedings of the SIGCHI Conference on Human Factors in Computing Systems*, pages 2139–2148. Copyright © 2009, Association for Computing Machinery, Inc. Reprinted by permission. DOI: 10.1145/1518701.1519026

Figure 42 from Wallace, et al: Investigating teamwork and taskwork in single- and multi-display groupware systems. *Personal and Ubiquitous Computing*, Volume 13, Issue 8, pages 569-581. Copyright © 2009, Springer Science+Business Media, LLC. Used with permission. DOI: 10.1007/s00779-009-0241-8

Figure 43 from Bachl, et al: The effects of personal displays and transfer techniques on collaboration strategies in multi-touch based multi-display environments. Human-Computer Interaction – INTERACT 2011: 13th IFIP TC 13 International Conference, Lisbon, Portugal, September 5-9, 2011, Proceedings, Part III, pages 373–390. Copyright © 2011 Springer-Verlag GmbH Berlin Heidelberg. Used with permission. DOI: 10.1007/978-3-642-23765-2_26

Figures 44a, b, c, d, e from Biehl, et al: Impromptu: A new interaction framework for supporting collaboration in multiple display environments and its field evaluation for co-located software development. *CHI '08 Proceedings of the SIGCHI Conference on Human Factors in Computing Systems*, pages 939–948. Copyright © 2008, Association for Computing Machinery, Inc. Reprinted by permission. DOI: 10.1145/1357054.1357200

Figure 45   from Haller, et al: The NiCE discussion room: Integrating paper and digital media to support co-located group meetings. *CHI '10 Proceedings of the SIGCHI Conference on Human Factors in Computing Systems*, pages 609-618. Copyright © 2010, Association for Computing Machinery, Inc. Reprinted by permission. DOI: 10.1145/1753326.1753418

Figure 46   from Liston, et al: Observations of two MEP iRoom coordination meetings: An investigation of artifact use in AEC project meetings. *CIFE Working Paper #WP106 from Stanford University* COPYRIGHT © 2007 by Center for Integrated Facility Engineering. Used with permission, http://cife.stanford.edu/sites/default/files/WP106.pdf

Figure 47   from Huang, et al: When design just isn't enough: The unanticipated challenges of the real world for large collaborative displays. *Personal and Ubiquitous Computing*, Volume 11, Issue 7, pages 537-547. Copyright © 2007, Springer Science+Business Media, LLC. Used with permission. DOI: 10.1007/s00779-006-0114-3

Figure 48   from Huang, et al: When design just isn't enough: The unanticipated challenges of the real world for large collaborative displays. *Personal and Ubiquitous Computing*, Volume 11, Issue 7, pages 537-547. Copyright © 2007 Springer-Verlag GmbH Berlin Heidelberg. Used with permission. DOI: 10.1007/s00779-006-0114-3

Figure 49   from Khan, et al: Toward the digital design studio: Large display explorations. *Human–Computer Interaction*, Volume 24, Issue 1-2, 2009, pages 9-47. © 2009 Taylor & Francis Group, LLC. Used with permission. DOI: 10.1080/07370020902819932

Figure 50   based on Scott, et al: Investigating tabletop interfaces to support collaborative decision-making in maritime operations. *Proceedings*, International Command and Control Research and Technology Symposium, 2010 and Scott and Allavena, Investigation of a prototype naval planning tool for tabletop computing research. *Report prepared for Defence Research and Development Canada - Atlanta, number CSL2010-01 in Collaborative Systems Laboratory*, pages 1–38, 2010.

Figures 51a, b, c   from Scott, et al: Investigating tabletop interfaces to support collaborative decision-making in maritime operations. *Proceedings*, International Command and Control Research and Technology Symposium, 2010. Used with permission, and Scott and Allavena, Investigation of a prototype naval planning tool for tabletop computing research. *Report prepared for Defence Research and Development Canada - Atlanta, number CSL2010-01 in Collaborative Systems Laboratory*, pages 1–38, 2010. Used with permission.

Figure 52   from Bederson, et al: Ordered and quantum treemaps: Making effective use of 2D space to display hierarchies. *ACM Transactions on Graphics*, 21(4):833–854, October 2002. Copyright © 2002, Association for Computing Machinery, Inc. Reprinted by permission. DOI: 10.1145/571647.571649

Figure 53   based on Amar and Stasko, Knowledge precepts for design and evaluation of information visualizations. *IEEE Transactions on Visualization and Computer Graphics*, 11(4):432–442, Jul.-Aug. 2005. Copyright © 2005 IEEE. Used with permission. DOI: 10.1109/TVCG.2005.63

Figure 54   based on Dörk, et al: The information flaneur: A fresh look at information seeking. *CHI '11 Proceedings of the SIGCHI Conference on Human Factors in Computing Systems*, pages 1215–1224. Copyright © 2011, Association for Computing Machinery, Inc. Reprinted by permission. DOI: 10.1145/1978942.1979124

Figure 55   based on Heuer, *Psychology of Intelligence Analysis*. Center for the Study of Intelligence, 1999. https://www.cia.gov/library/center-for-the-study-of-intelligence/csi-publications/books-and-monographs/psychology-of-intelligence-analysis/index.html

Figure 56   from Nobarany, et al: Facilitating the reuse process in distributed collaboration: A distributed cognition approach. *CSCW '12 Proceedings of the ACM 2012 conference on Computer Supported Cooperative Work*, pages 1223-1232. Copyright © 2012, Association for Computing Machinery, Inc. Reprinted by permission. DOI: 10.1145/2145204.2145388

Figure 57   based on Posner and Rothbart, Research on attention networks as a model for the integration of psychological science. *Annual Review of Psychology*, 58: 1-23, 2007. First published online as a *Review in Advance* on October 9, 2006. DOI: 10.1146/annurev.psych.58.110405.085516

Figure 58   The Tobii Glasses Eye Tracker. Copyright © 2013 Tobii Technology. Used with permission, `http://www.tobii.com/en/eye-tracking-research/global/products/hardware/tobii-glasses-eye-tracker/`

Figures 59a, b   from Freeth, et al: Do gaze cues in complex scenes capture and direct the attention of high functioning adolescents with ASD? Evidence from eye- tracking. *Journal of Autism and Developmental Disorders*, Volume 40, Issue 5, pages 534-547. Copyright © 2009, Springer Science+Business Media, LLC. Used with permission. DOI: 10.1007/s10803-009-0893-2

Figure 60   from Chetwood, et al: Collaborative eye tracking: A potential training tool in laparoscopic surgery. *Surgical Endoscopy*, Volume 26, Issue 7, pages 1–7. Copyright © 2012, Springer Science+Business Media, LLC. Used with permission. DOI: 10.1007/s00464-011-2143-x

Figure 61   based on Duffy, Situation awareness analysis and measurement. *Human Factors and Ergonomics in Manufacturing & Service Industries*, 11(4):383 –384, 2001. Copyright © 2001 John Wiley & Sons, Inc. DOI: 10.1002/hfm.1021

Figure 62   based on Salerno, et al: Building a framework for situation awareness. *Proceedings of the 7th International Conference on Information Fusion*, 2004. `http://www.fusion2004.foi.se/papers/IF04-0219.pdf`

Figure 63   based on Yin, et al: VisFlowConnect: Netflow visualizations of link relationships for security situational awareness. *VizSEC/DMSEC '04 Proceedings of the 2004 ACM workshop on Visualization and data mining for computer security*, pages 26–34. Copyright © 2004, Association for Computing Machinery, Inc. DOI: 10.1145/1029208.1029214 and Yurcik, Tool update: Visflowconnect-IP with advanced filtering from usability testing. *VizSEC '06 Proceedings of the 3rd international workshop on Visualization for computer security*, pages 63–64. Copyright © 2006, Association for Computing Machinery, Inc. DOI: 10.1145/1179576.1179588

Figure 64 based on Diseree Sy. Adapting usability investigations for agile user-centered design. *Journal of Usability Studies*, 2(3):112–132, May 2007. http://www.upassoc.org/upa_publications/jus/2007may/agile-ucd.html

Figure 65 MultiTaction Cell Ultra Thin Bezel. Copyright © 2013 MultiTouch Ltd. Used with permission.

Figure 66 based on Kivy Architecture, http://kivy.org/#home

Figure 67a from Reas and Fry, *Getting started with processing: A quick, hands-on introduction*. Make Series. O'Reilly Media, 2010. Published by Maker Media, Inc. Print ISBN: 978-1-4493-7980-3. Used with permission.

Figure 67b from Kuckuck, Realtime Information Graphics at Telekom Product Experience Center, from Atelier Markgraph with Zum Kuckuck / Büro für digitale Medien. Available at: http://projects.zumkuckuck.com/realtime/ and http://markgraph.de/de/flash.html#/257/cGlkKzEwMDAvc29ydG8rL3NvcnRmK2NhdGVnb3J5/ Used with permission.

Figure 68 based onMulti-touch application, MT4j architecture. http://mt4j.org/mediawiki/index.php/Main_Page

CHAPTER 1

Purpose and Direction

1.1 INTRODUCTION

Surfaces are non-traditional digital displays allowing direct interaction with the surface of the display by supporting pen or touch input (especially multi-touch input), and 2D gesture recognition. A full discussion on what we mean by surfaces will be provided in chapter 2 where we will predominantly discuss *large multi-touch surfaces* (large vertical or tabletop displays). These increasingly available, affordable, and under-utilized surfaces can be used to gather a group of people around a single interactive display to support their collaborative work. We also discuss how other types of surfaces, such as tablets, smartphones, or regular displays can play important secondary roles in supporting collaborative work. Regardless of the type of surface, we are especially interested in *interactions* with surface technologies, and present many systems, including our own, that have been developed to explore this space.

We will define *collaboration*, a remarkably vague term [73], more tightly in chapter 4, but for now we give a brief introduction. The term is used in different ways when organizations collaborate with each other, i.e., inter-agency collaboration, compared to when it is used to describe the work of small groups whose members all belong to the same organization. In this book, we primarily discuss *small group intra-agency collaboration*. In this context, collaboration is generally understood as the activity of a group of people (often called a team) who are jointly working toward a common purpose, and whose work is interdependent. To be clear, not all types of small group work is collaborative work [150][53], and we primarily explore the value of surfaces to collaborative teams. In particular, we explore *collaborative analytic activity*, i.e., groups of analysts who have a joint goal, whose work is intense, and who depend upon one another to complete their overall activity. The interdependence arises because "the value of the contributions that each member makes to the group product, depends in part on contributions made by other members" (Straus & McGrath) [190]. We explore the value of surfaces for this type of analytic team.

In trying to grapple with how surfaces can support collaborating analysts we will spend some time exploring the nature of collaborative analytic work. We will often use theory to do this. For example, McGrath created a taxonomy of eight different types of collaborative activity [135]. Within his taxonomy, the types of group activities of primary relevance to *collaborative analysis work* are intellective tasks and decision-making tasks, both of which are judgment tasks characterized as 'choosing' processes that require group members to work interdependently. We think theory, such as McGrath's taxonomy, provides valuable insight. In this case we find the theory useful as a reminder of the innate nature of analytic work and its ambiguities, explaining the need for ample team discussions and explorations of data. We think theory can lead to useful questions (many of which are still unanswered or only partially answered), such as "How can surfaces support analytic teams in the process of making choices?"

We believe there are many ways that the various phases of collaborative analysis work can be supported by surfaces [73] [49][64]. We know that collaborative work in general requires significant amounts of communication (talking and sharing of artifacts), coordination (the inter-weaving of the various work strands) and cooperation (when team members work toward a joint goal) [135][190]. Most of the surface systems presented in this book support collaborative work in its cooperative phase, and to a lesser degree in its coordinative phases.

Like other collaborative activities, collaborative analytic work can occur across the usual space and time continua [73], i.e., collaboration may involve groups who may or may not be co-located or working synchronously. This book emphasizes co-located analysis teams, who are working synchronously around tabletops or large displays.

There is some indication that at least some of the aspects of the type of collaborative work we are studying occur best when co-located and synchronous, i.e., face-to-face. In the context of an investigation of this issue, Straus and McGrath studied groups engaged in tasks that were either of low (e.g., idea generation tasks), medium (e.g., intellective tasks) or high (e.g., judgment tasks) interdependence. They observed 72 groups working face-to-face or at a distance through simple text-based conferencing software and concluded that for judgment tasks especially, there was a big discrepancy between those who worked face-to-face versus those who worked through computer media with respect to overall effectiveness. They found that in general "face-to-face modes are superior to computer-mediated discussions when productivity is a priority or when the time available to perform tasks is at a premium, especially for highly interdependent tasks" [190]. In addition they found that for intellective tasks and judgment tasks, face-to-face encounters were significantly more satisfying. While this is a pursuasive argument for not using chat technologies for collaborative analytic work, researchers do not really know if surface technologies will enable collaborative analytic work as well as pure face-to-face collaboration. Using common sense we would hope that surface technologies would provide all the value of face-to-face collaboration, but that surfaces would also add additional value. However, this particular study has yet to be conducted. This discussion raises two themes that run throughout this book. The first is that there are many unanswered questions in this research area. The second is the importance of design.

We believe that in ideal circumstances, well-designed collaborative technologies that can bring people and artifacts together (such as large displays, large surfaces or systems of surfaces) are important enablers of collaborative actions and an important part of supporting expert behavior in complex practices. However, we also acknowledge that real life is very complex. Face-to-face interactions are not always possible, and not always ideal [83].

In our studies we have found that in practice much work is a mixture of face-to-face and at-a-distance collaboration, which can be wholly satisfactory. In addition, we have found that real collaborative analysis work can be a mixture of collaborative and individual efforts, and that, to add to the complexity, often collaborative, co-located, synchronous work can be a mixture of face-to-face and side-by-side collaboration (we've heard this type of co-located collaboration described as mixed-focus collaboration). This variety suggests that no one form of collaboration is best, nor is there one best technological solution. With respect to surfaces, we explore their many variations. For example, although it would initially appear that horizontal surfaces might only enable face-to-face collaboration, in fact it is possible to link two distant tables to bring disparate team members together enabling both face-to-face and at-a-distance simultaneously. The same can be said for vertical surfaces.

We next discuss a few aspects of collaborative analytic work that are emerging trends, which helps to explain why surface technologies may be a suitable technology to enable it.

1.2   TRENDS IN ANALYSIS WORK AND SURFACES TECHNOLOGIES

Analysts in many domains are faced with larger amounts of data to analyze. In the extreme case, this huge and growing volume of data together with increased complexity through internal and external semantic connectivity is often called *big data* [20]. This extreme case is a complex topic [66], which we do not address in this book.

However, even when this extreme case is not being considered, it is increasingly unrealistic to analyze data directly, i.e., by looking at its raw source, be it quantitative or qualitative, because there is simply too much of it, and because most of it is 'noise.' An early book by Tukey encouraged analysts to summarize data sets to formulate hypotheses [207]. Subsequently, Cleveland, who considered computer-generated visualizations, encouraged analysts to use these visualizations to take advantage of the holistic view that they provide to explore the structure of data and to check the validity of statistical results [41]. Most recently, Tufte has produced a series of books to address the topic of visualizations as aids to thinking [204] and as a means of depicting evidence that evokes a reaction [205, 206]. Many of the systems we discuss in chapter 2 employ information visualization techniques, although some use scientific visualizations.

Despite the obvious challenges posed by designing visualizations well, today more and more analysts rely on visualizations of data obtained from large databases to quickly understand large data sets, to identify areas of interest, and to explore those interests based on hypotheses they are building about the data. Because of the way visualizations are typically designed, analysts also use them as a way to access detailed data. Our emphasis will be more about issues to do with interacting with visualizations, rather than their production because we feel visualizing and interacting with visualizations can enable intellective and decision-making group processes. While humans have natural abilities to recognize patterns and anomalies in the data, to derive meaning from these occurrences, and to form hypotheses and test their understandings, interacting with such visualizations provides further advantages, in particular because it enables exploration.

Analysis work is also becoming more complex because analysts seldom analyze single data sets, but are merging data sets and making associations across them.

Emerging challenges in the analysis domain are driving *collaborative analysis work* toward becoming the norm, since a single analyst cannot necessarily complete complex tasks in the time required, or because analysts from multiple domains are required to merge their areas of expertise in a combined effort to complete a joint analysis task.

Collaborative work poses additional challenges to data analysis. Some of these challenges can simply be mitigated by additional screen real-estate (pixels), allowing the work artifacts (the documents, visualizations, lists and so on) of one or more analysts to be laid side-by-side for visual inspection. However, software tools designed to produce visualizations or interact with visualizations are not necessarily able to support collaborative analysis tasks easily because they have often been designed with the assumption that the analysis will be conducted by a single person who will interact with the data using a traditional desktop display, mouse and keyboard. Even tools that *do* assume face-to-face collaboration do *not* assume their output will be on large surfaces, or that interaction will occur through non-standard means such as touch, multi-touch or pen.

While it is possible to conduct collaborative analysis work with tools that are designed to be driven by one user controlling the action with a mouse, this approach can and should be challenged, if for no other reason than to break down the inefficiencies that are imposed by this approach. Furthermore, even if a single analyst is using a large surface to lay out their work arti-facts, mice interactions may prove to be more awkward than touch. For these reasons and others, we examine natural user interface paradigms [223].

Other issues introduced when work becomes collaborative is organizing the task, support-ing parallel work, and keeping the various parties involved in the analysis work aware of the progress being made. Computers can help here and in particular, large displays can facilitate the coordination of the various tasks involved in collaborative work because visualizations of the tasks can easily be displayed to the members of the analysis team.

In some domains there is also increasing pressure to analyze large amounts of data very quickly or nearly in real time (as the data arrives). Analysis of this type of data is always challeng-ing, but collaborative real-time analysis work has its own unique sets of pressures that include and extend beyond those of non real-time collaborative analysis work. In these circumstances it is likely much more important that the work be tightly coordinated and that all the analysts are aware of the work of others for the joint task to proceed smoothly. These conditions present unique challenges to designers creating software systems. Computer systems and well-designed visualizations of the work can facilitate this awareness.

1.3   OBJECTIVE OF THE BOOK

We hope to stimulate the discussion on how to meet the demands introduced by the need to analyze large and diverse data sets. The changes required are various; they touch on many aspects of analysis work, such as cultural practices, how analyses are conducted, the physical spaces in the buildings, and the software and hardware systems employed in collaborative, multi-disciplinary analysis work. Our aim is to explore the role that surfaces may play in evolving analysis work to confront problems that arise from challenges presented by large data sets. In particular we address the pros and cons of using large surfaces to support collaborative analysis work involving large amounts of data. We also provide a sense of the 'state of the art' of these displays and the advances being made to make surfaces effective collaboration tools. Throughout we consider the issues, challenges, and potential for developing the computer systems that are required to support challenging collaborative analysis tasks, emphasizing the role of design in achieving this objective.

Many outstanding questions remain, and important early studies have pointed out some challenges. For example, there are many advocates of a 'natural' interaction style, but Yuill and Rogers have questioned what is understood by this construct. They have suggested that the so-called 'natural' interactions afforded by surface technologies are not a given, but must be consciously designed with a deep understanding of appropriate constraints on an activity [234]. This theme of the advantages of surfaces being conditional on design considerations runs throughout this book. Wherever possible, we highlight design lessons learned thus far.

1.4   STRUCTURE OF THE BOOK

Chapter 2 reviews systems that capitalize on surface technologies (large display surfaces and systems of surfaces) to visualize and interact with large amounts of data. We emphasize interactions with visualizations, since our understanding is that analysis work is accomplished by enabling exploration of data, exploiting the strengths of both computer systems and human analysts. We consider systems with two different types of data sources: large databases and to a lesser extent, network streamed data. We consider how the problem of large data sets has been addressed in a variety of analytic domains. We also draw attention to systems that are able to deal with network streamed data.

Chapter 3 discusses new interaction issues that arise when interacting with large surfaces or systems of surfaces. These issues are at the root of some of the impedances to social interaction that will be identified in chapter 4. These include issues such as the ability to point at objects, the ability to move information between displays, and the design of gestural systems for multi-person multi-touch systems. Our goal is to review the rapid advancements being made in these areas.

The pros and cons of using surface technologies to support collaborative work are reviewed in chapter 4. We discuss research on the positive aspects of using surface technologies, such as the ability of large surfaces to support teams to coordinate their work and also to invite and enable the simultaneous engagement of team members. Research on the challenges introduced when using surface applications in group contexts are also addressed. This includes the difficulties that arise when laying out and arranging work objects, or pointing at objects when surfaces are large and parts of it are out of an individual's reach. We also look at these issues in terms of how social interaction can be impeded if surface systems are poorly designed.

Chapter 5 addresses the topic of theory. We define the collaborative analysis task more specifically and review some useful theoretical paradigms for understanding collaborative work, such as distributed cognition, evolutionary psychology, group situation awareness, a psychophys-iological perspective on attention, and activity theory. We present theories and paradigms that help to understand the behavior and cognitive functioning of analyst teams. When team or group work becomes more important, then broader theories beyond those that explain individual be-haviors also begin to have value. We provide many concrete examples of how understandings of teams and groups has guided the development of tools for collaborating analysts.

Chapter 6 reviews useful high-level architectural knowledge for developing surface appli-cations. These include interaction patterns that have been observed by researchers studying col-laborators using surface technologies, systems and development environments for creating surface technologies, software architectures for multi-surface collaborative applications, and methods for developing surface applications. This section is based on our lab's experience developing prototype applications for large vertical surfaces, and mixed-display environments including displays, large surfaces, tablets and smartphones.

Chapter 7 summarizes our findings and summarizes the challenges and opportunities for research identified in the previous chapters.

CHAPTER 2

Surface Technologies and Collaborative Analysis Systems

In this chapter we first focus on large surface technologies, emphasizing those that have gone beyond the research lab and have become widely available. We then consider systems designed for analysis of large-scale data, especially where the analysis involves large-scale displays and collaboration. Our goal is to position these two elements, surface technologies for their potential to transform system design, and existing collaborative analysis systems to show the current state of practice.

2.1   SURFACE TECHNOLOGIES

We have claimed that *surfaces* are non-traditional digital displays allowing direct interaction with the surface of the display by supporting pen or touch input, especially multi-touch input, and 2D gesture recognition. However, this is an area of rapid change, both in the technology itself, and in the conceptualization of the design opportunities. Therefore the definition of surfaces and opportunities are both in flux. For example, surface computing involves some technologies that work best for small-scale displays and others for large-scale displays, but the boundaries are changing. Touch input can be accomplished using fingers or specially designed pens that simulate finger touches, but some surface systems are created with specially designed pens and paper or projectors and cameras, and these do not require a traditional display. Each of these configurations presents different opportunities to designers.

We emphasize the role of surfaces in the context of activities, but others emphasize the role of gestures (at or above the surface), graphical feedback or navigation styles that work with gestures. Such ideas are the basis of models such as 'reality-based interaction' [98], and the increasing popularity of the term 'Natural User Interfaces' [99, 223] even though others have urged caution about the term 'natural,' noting that both habituation and design are very much involved [127, 148, 234].

In using the term "surface computing," we stress the importance of 2D gesture interaction on the surface. Some gestures have become widely accepted, such as zoom-out (pinch fingers on surface) and pan object (drag finger across surface). Gestures are typically recognized by software once touch events have been detected, and there is the potential to detect a variety of kinds of gestures, and even to allow definition and customization of gestures. We concentrate mostly on surface computing where input is done via fingertip with multi-touch capability and simple fingertip gesture recognition, which is now a built-in feature of many commercial devices.

There are many other possibilities for surface input. Some devices can track not just fingertips, but also hand postures, hand parts, finger postures and even finger tips. Other systems require special gloves that enable surface applications to distinguish knuckles, palms, sides and backs of hands, creating the possibility for very expressive gestural systems [129, 129]. There are also other ways to interact with surface technologies including the use of pens, tangibles, styluses, or various long-distance pointing devices [34].

Our focus is on technologies that are commonplace and pragmatic. In our research we want to consider applications of the technology, especially for collaborative analysis, rather than the technology itself. We are motivated by the recent affordability of large multi-touch displays. Moreover, multi-touch overlays are now available that can convert large flat-panel displays into multi-touch surfaces. Also, projection systems are dropping in price, and small multi-touch surfaces, such as Apple's iOS devices and Google Android devices, are becoming ubiquitous. The increasing affordability and availability of these devices is a significant opportunity.

However, while developments at the hardware level have been rapid, application software for large surface technologies is still in the early stages. The main area of design and development has been productivity apps, utilities and games for the small hand-held iOS and Android devices. For large surfaces, the application software that is most widely used is the software that is shipped with the hardware, and it is principally used for demonstration purposes.

In our view, this represents an opportunity to design new 'killer apps' that are perfectly suited to large surface technology. We are encouraged in this regard, by early results that have already shown that surfaces can help groups make sense of data [156]. We speculate that surface computing enables novel and strong support for group work and collaboration, and that the more data-centric the collaborative work, the more valuable multi-touch surfaces might become. In the subsections below, we first outline relevant technologies, and then relevant surface applications for analysts.

2.1.1   LARGE SURFACES: OPTICAL TOUCH RECOGNITION

Large surface displays typically use some form of computer vision to resolve touch coordinates. The technique popularized by Jeff Han [79] and then immortalized on CNN for the 2008 U.S. presidential election is called Frustrated Total Internal Reflection (FTIR) (Figure 2.1(a)). Beams of infrared light are shone into the edge of a clear acrylic display. The light beams skip along inside the acrylic until a finger deforms one side of the display. At that point the beams are projected down into a video camera filtered to only detect infrared light.

Diffuse Illumination (DI) (Figure 2.1(b)) is similar to FTIR in that it uses infrared light. The difference is that infrared illumination bathes the underside of the translucent display, reflecting finger touches as they flatten on the glass. This bath of light provides an opportunity for detection of fiducial markers, which are physical objects, possibly with distinctive marks, posi-

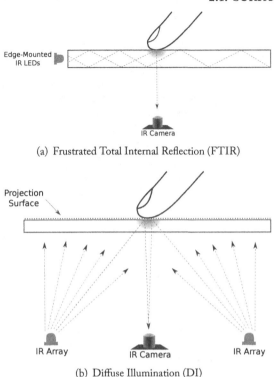

(a) Frustrated Total Internal Reflection (FTIR)

(b) Diffuse Illumination (DI)

Figure 2.1: Detecting touches. Optical multi-touch technologies.

tioned on and interacting with surfaces. Fiducial markers are described in more detail in a section below.

With its ability to detect numerous simultaneous touch points and its large surface area, Han's design was immediately considered a potential collaboration tool. However, it should be noted that Han's FTIR displays take up a fairly large footprint. The requirement for cameras and projectors can lead to a proportionally large installation behind or below the display. Nevertheless, SMART Technologies and Microsoft both produced well-engineered and widely distributed commercial products based on this design. The SMART Table, and the Microsoft Surface are shown in Figure 2.2.

Both DI and FTIR use infrared sensitive cameras to detect touches, with a visible light projector displaying the image. Both camera and projector must be able to reach the whole screen, so both are mounted some distance beneath the screen, hence the requirement for a large and deep housing.

More recently, Microsoft also introduced a product, which was originally called Surface 2.0. The hardware is manufactured and marketed by Samsung as the SUR40 and includes the

(a) Smart Table (Source: www.smarttech.com)

(b) MS Surface 1.0
(Source: technet.microsoft.com)

(c) MS PixelSense and Samsung SUR40 (Source:
samsung.com)

Figure 2.2: Commercial touch solutions.

Microsoft technology called PixelSense. The hardware is a 40-inch diagonal liquid crystal display, backed by a large grid of simple sensors that allow the detection of touches and objects on or slightly over the surface of the display. This approach is still essentially optical, but the sensors can be embedded in a layer behind the display screen, eliminating the need for the depth requirement associated with DI or FTIR approaches. This allows the SUR40 to be used as a conventional table, with empty space beneath, or it can be a wall-mounted display.

Another approach to achieving a thin display is to mount infrared lights and detectors along the same plane as the surface, around the edge of the unit, and just slightly above the display itself. This technology is typically embedded in a frame. A number of proprietary multi-touch systems have reached the market using this technique, with SMART Technologies and PQ Labs offering their own touch-detecting frames, and also licensing the technology for use in other products. These approaches result in a thin frame that can be used with a conventional flat display. The frame sizes are scalable, ranging from desktop screens to wall displays. However, there are limitations on the number of independent touch events that can be resolved.

The key enabling technology for large surfaces is multi-touch recognition without inconvenient side-effects or unacceptably high cost. The technologies we have reviewed above are the those that have successfully been deployed in widespread commercial products. However, active research in this area is ongoing, and new approaches and prototypes are still appearing. Moreover, there are many commercial products available that we have not described because they are offered on a smaller scale or custom-built, typically either for research or for use in high-impact trade displays.

2.1.2   SMALL SURFACES: ELECTRONIC TOUCH RECOGNITION

Multi-touch surfaces also use a variety of non-optical technologies to capture user input. Two technologies are common: capacitive and resistive screens. Capacitive screens use the conductive properties of human fingers or specially designed styluses to resolve points of contact. The resolution is moderately precise and the very light pressure required for activation creates an impression of responsiveness. Resistive screens are reported to be slightly less responsive, but they can be activated by any object and they have the advantage of greater accuracy, especially when a stylus is used. Unfortunately both capacitive and resistive screen sizes are difficult to manufacture at larger than handheld screen dimensions. However, at those smaller sizes, they allow robust and relatively inexpensive products. This is the approach typically used on devices such as smartphones (e.g., iPhone, Android phones) or tablets (e.g., iPad, Android tablets).

Another important technology that enables surface computing involves electronic 'pens.' Probably the most widely explored technology is that of the Swedish company Anoto. Anoto technology involves special pens that work together with special, almost imperceptible dot patterns that are printed on a paper surface. Anoto pens include a small camera near the tip, and the position of the pen can be determined by analysis of the pattern seen by the camera. The uniqueness of the dot patterns can be maintained over large wall-sized areas (Figure 4.11 in section 4.4.5), enabling an excellent combination of precision and range. The exact coordinates are transmitted via Bluetooth to the computer projecting the updated display. The precision is fine enough to enable handwriting recognition and the conversion of rough drawings to formal diagrams. The large surface area supported by Anoto makes it ideal for collaboration [78]. Multiple pens can be distinguished, and the fact that each pen is distinct also allows for personalized interfaces and menus based on the pen's (and by extension the pen holder's) identity.

2.1.3 INTERACTION BEYOND THE SURFACE

While we regard the detection of multiple touches to be the key enabler of surface computing, some technologies also allow capabilities beyond the surface. For tables this means above the table, and for wall displays it means in the space directly in front. There are several approaches that are currently available.

Fiducial markers: As we discussed above, several technologies for touch detection involve computer vision, where touches are seen directly by cameras or visual sensors. The principal use is detection of fingertips on the exterior of the display surface. However, some technologies can be used to visually detect other artifacts positioned on the surface exterior.

The most common approach is to identify artifacts by visual markings known as fiducials positioned on the bottom of the artifacts where they are in contact with the surface (Figure 2.3). The fiducials can then be identified by the visual system, and their identity can be determined by the computer.

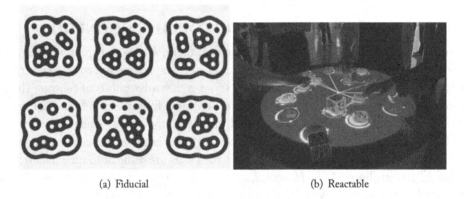

(a) Fiducial   (b) Reactable

Figure 2.3: Tangible User Interfaces. Sources: reactivision.sourceforge.net, Wikimedia Commons

This approach is possible with surfaces using DI or hybrid FTIR/DI designs, because the infrared camera can see through the transparent surface, without interaction from the visible light from the projected image. The approach is also possible using MS PixelSense on the Samsung SUR40, because the light sensors can also detect visual patterns on the exterior of the screen. The interaction paradigm that is facilitated by this technology allows users to manipulate 3D artifacts on the surface, where the identity and the position of each artifact can be determined by the computer. This allows the users to work with physical tokens that represent objects, actions, filters, and so on. The paradigm resembles that of tangible user interfaces (TUIs), where the interaction is directly mediated by manipulated artifacts. For more on TUIs, see the survey by Shaer and Hornecker [180].

TUIs make it possible for users to interact with a system by manipulating objects in the real world. This can be seen, as Hornecker says [85], as simply "giving physical form to digital information", or it can be seen as something much more. Hornecker's awareness of additional dimensions of TUIs in collaborative settings helps explain the interaction more completely. She finds that in the literature for tangible interaction "we can distinguish a data-centered view, pursued in Computer Science and HCI; an expressive-movement-centered view from Industrial and Product Design; and a space-centered view influenced from Arts and Architecture" [84]. This perspective offers an important framework for considering the representational and social effects of this interaction type.

The capabilities of fiducial markers on a surface are somewhat more limited because they only convey identity and position, but the overall approach appears to allow interfaces to be created at a lower cost and with greater flexibility than with fully-fledged TUIs. The research work on TUIs, together with growing availability of surfaces with fiducial capabilities, appears to offer opportunities for more widespread exploration. The recent work by Spindler et al. [187] outlines the potential of this approach; we discuss this more below.

Augmented reality: While fiducial markers principally enable input using artifacts beyond the surface, another technology allows output beyond the surface, allowing a kind of *bidirectionally*.

Augmented reality (AR) is a type of interface that combines digital objects and information with reality. In particular, one approach to AR involves external cameras and computer vision to detect markers in a real-world view, and general computer imagery aligned with those markers to create an augmented view of the world. The view is updated in real time, allowing the generated imagery to move, for example, to reflect changing position or perspective. To view the augmented display, users can wear transparent head-mounted displays coupled with cameras, where the display shows the real world-view with the augmented imagery overlaid. Alternatively, users can look at/through external monitors or mobile displays that show the augmented view from the position of fixed or mobile cameras.

There are various ways in which AR can work with surfaces. For example, the markers can be physical objects with fiducial markers on both sides, one for the surface computer, and one for the AR display. Alternatively, fiducial markers can be displayed on the surface itself, and the AR display can then represent the markers with generated imagery. In either case, 3D virtual objects are shown with the perspective changing as the user moves the surface around in space (Figure 2.4(b)).

To consider what such AR systems are like, imagine moving around a room using a tablet computer as a smart lens into a landscape, seeing—and perhaps filtering or selecting—details that

(a) ARTag Detection of fiducial markers

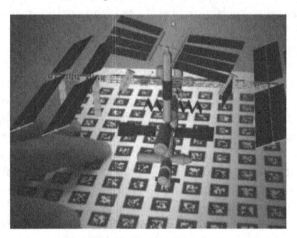

(b) ARTag 3D Augmentation of reality

Figure 2.4: ARTag "Magic Lens" Augmented surfaces. Virtual objects, games, and animations appear to enter the real world when seen through a variety of displays. Source: www.artag.net

are hidden to the naked eye. Part of the appeal of prototypes built with this technology is in their novelty, but we do see the potential for practical uses in analysis and visualization similar to the Magic Lens idea (Figure 2.20). For example, three-dimensional representations of dense information could be easily viewed from any angle or depth, and with the user physically moving around the visualization, their spatial relationship to the data could enhance their understanding of it. For a less abstract example, a city map could be represented in 3D and overlaid with municipal services information. Numerous other examples can be found in the work of Billinghurst [39].

Movement beyond the surface: Our scope is surface computing, and we emphasize the nature of interaction with the surface. In our discussions of fiducial markers and augmented reality, we still concentrate on their detection and display on the exterior of the surface. However, it is also possible to allow interaction well beyond the surface itself.

Several technologies have been widely used for interacting with surfaces from across room-size distances. Their principle deployment is for console games, and the devices used are the Sony Eyetoy, the Nintendo Wiimote, and the Microsoft Kinect.

The Sony EyeToy works with the Sony Playstation 2, and its successor, the Playstation Eye, works with the Playstation 3. The Playstation Eye is a simple video camera pointed at the user in the space in front of the display. The main approach used is computer vision, which is used to detect shape and movement based on a simple model of a human silhouette. The location and speed of the movement is used as input to the game.

The Nintendo Wiimote is used with the Nintendo Wii. The user holds the Wiimote in their hand, moving it and sometimes pointing it at the screen. There are two methods of input: one is accomplished by reading the accelerometer data from the device, and the other is based on computer vision from an infrared camera at the front of the device, which is used to detect the location of the screen, or rather the infrared lights on a sensor bar located near the display. These allow the device to be used to gesture toward imagery on the display, giving the illusion of interaction with the display by pointing.

The Microsoft Kinect is used with the Microsoft XBox 360. The Microsoft Kinect is positioned near the display, and includes both an infrared projector and infrared camera. The projector emits a continuous stream of structured infrared light over the three dimensional area in front of the screen. The camera sees the pattern on the infrared light reflected off anything in the room, and a computer vision system compares captured patterns to infer 3D shapes. The shapes are principally that of the users, which are interpreted using models of human skeletal articulation. This allows the detection of gestures and directions indicated by movement of the user's arms, head and legs.

New applications written for the Kinect input device are appearing every day. For instance MIT's Tangible Media group has produced a prototype called Kinected Conference [54] that augments video conferencing with each speaker's identity, the amount of time each person has spent speaking, the ability for a person to temporarily hide from the camera without leaving their place, and the ability to interact with augmented reality objects.

2.2 SYSTEMS FOR COLLABORATIVE ANALYSIS

A number of approaches can be taken when considering the use of surface applications for analysts. One area is the visualization of large data sets. This general area began with scientific visualization (where visual presentations typically utilize spatial relationships underlying the phenomena of interest) and then progressed to information visualization (where the visual presentation typically involves more abstract structures) [35]. Both areas use principles of visual perception to distinguish and relate elements, dimensions, and relationships in the data. Both scientific and information visualization can assist in a variety of activities, in particular supporting both the presentation of already understood phenomena, and the identification and understanding of new phenomena [35]. A more recent approach that has been distinguished is that of *visual analytics*, where a range of disciplines, still including those interested in visual perception, but also now including individuals interested in problem-solving processes, aim to assist in analysis activities [195, 228]. Although traditionally concerned only with visual displays, those interested in visual analytics are beginning to see there is greater value in interactive visualizations.

Isenberg et al. [94] have shown that in the domain of collaborative visualization analysis, research over a 10-year span clearly indicates a growing emphasis on large displays and collaborative work. In particular, the number of papers published on collaborative face-to-face analysis in three major venues (IEEE Conference on Visualization, IEEE Conference on Information Visualization, and Visual Analytics Science and Technology) has risen (Figure 2.5).

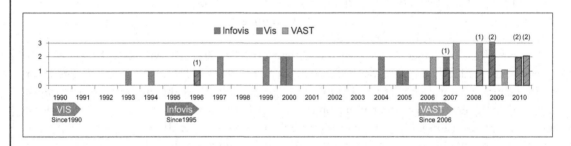

Figure 2.5: Number of research papers on large displays and collaborative systems from 1990-2010. Papers published in IEEE Vis, InfoVis and VAST have seen tremendous growth in recent years; shading and numbers above a bar indicate numbers of co-located, as opposed to at-a-distance papers on collaboration. Source: based on [94]

Large non-interactive displays have frequently been used for collaboration purposes and we provide an interesting review of targeted uses for large displays in the analysis domain [29].

2.2.1   LARGE DISPLAYS AND COLLABORATION

Perhaps the most immediate link between display technology and collaboration involves large screens. Large displays allow several people to see detail and to point at features and discuss them—even if there is no interaction with any software.

Of course, many large screen systems are not intended for this, and may simply be meant to facilitate single users. With affordable flat-screen displays and multi-display video cards, large displays for single users are common and growing. For example, the VAST 2009 Traffic Mini Challenge involved a design challenge to help an analyst find a security threat in the provided data. One response featured a large tiled display consisting of eight 30 inch LCD panels, like in Figure 2.6, oriented for use by a single analyst.

Figure 2.6: An eight x 30-inch LCD tiled display shown in the 2009 VAST Traffic Mini Challenge. Source: [61]

For real collaboration, analysts working together in either co-located or distributed settings have a need to interact easily with data and with each other—needs that have been identified and explored by the research community. Collaboration may include the ability to create separate views, which each analyst can then annotate and comment on, or perhaps separate workspaces that allow each analyst to view data in their own way. As an example of such a system, Isenberg et al. describes a 'Command Post of the Future' (CPOF), which involves a networked visualization display where commanders are able to create their own analysis views by dragging and dropping their analysis into a public view (Figure 2.7) [94].

One simple approach to using large displays for analysis work is to use established visualization systems at a larger scale. For example, Best and colleagues developed MeDECi, a platform for high-throughput processing, for a government department processing hundreds of millions to billions of transactions per day [19]. Tools like Clique and Traffic Circles, built on this framework, provide high and low level near 'real-time' visualizations of network flows that have been collected

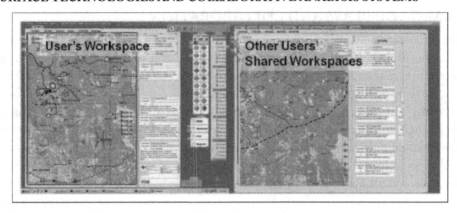

Figure 2.7: Private and shared workspaces. Analysts can create their own workspaces (left) while multiple analysts can share a workspace (right). Source: [94]

by MeDECi. These tools receive streaming data from MeDECi and then provide streaming analytics. Clique and Traffic Circles are illustrated in Figure 2.8 and analysts viewing Traffic Circles on a large display are shown in Figure 2.9.

A more elaborate approach is simply to use the same kind of multi-screen high-resolution display, but support some kind of analysis involving several members of a collaborative team. For example, this is what is done in a recent system described for x-ray radiography analysis [229]. By providing the analysts with a very large surface to view, manipulate, annotate, and markup x-ray images, they are able to view very fine details without losing the big picture. In addition, they are able to lay related images side by side while retaining the ability to markup and look between them. In Figure 2.10 an analyst examines the X-ray image of a gas turbine on the HIPerSpace tiled display. The display is 70 networked 30-inch LCD displays offering approximately 286 mega-pixel resolution.

Another example of using large displays for group analysis work comes from structural biology. Bryden et al. developed a system for displaying large protein structures, which enables biologists to easily point, manipulate, and collaboratively analyze the structures [33]. Typically, protein structures are quite massive and are hard to analyze, especially when exploring how they fit with other protein structures. Figure 2.11 shows how current large displays are used by biologists without refined interaction techniques. In order to overcome pointing issues with the current large displays, the method of input was abstracted out so that in theory any device which interfaces with their system could be applied. Bryden et al. acknowledge that touch would be a good solution for their system, though they used Wiimote and the Xbox dual-stick controllers.

As a final example, Bradel et al. demonstrate that large high-resolution displays can play a key role in improving co-located collaborative sensemaking, particularly for intelligence purposes [28]. Sensemaking refers to the act of foraging, filtering and extracting useful information while

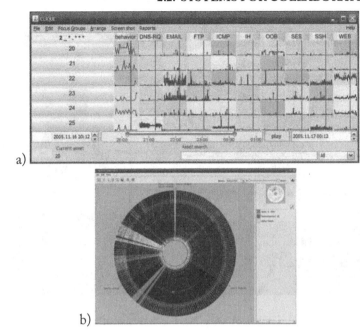

Figure 2.8: Visualizations for analyzing networked streamed data. a) The Clique system learns what is anomalous in flows of data. It displays compact time lines for machines and ports. Controls allow analysts to play and replay the data as well as select networks and ports of interest. b) A large Traffic Circle display captures 125 million flows using a high-performance database to allow for interactivity. Analysts can get more data on anomalous flows by pointing at a flow. Source: [19]

Figure 2.9: Analyzing networked streamed data using a large display. Analysts explore data flows using a Traffic Circle visualization on a large display. Source: [19]

Figure 2.10: HIPerspace tiled display. A very large interactive display used to analyze the digital X-ray of a small gas turbine. Source: [229]

Figure 2.11: Biologists examine protein structures on a large display. There is room for improvement in current visualization tools. It is not easy to point when engaging with the system shown above. Source: [33]

Figure 2.12: uMeeting: A tabletop display system. The uTable, which is part of the uMeeting system, is a rear-projected multi-touch display. Source: [124]

generating potential schemas and hypotheses. Intelligence refers to the information, i.e., the raw data, documents and reports of various incidents around the world, that are used for the purpose of ensuring the safety of a country's citizens. In Bradel et al.'s system, analysts are co-located and leverage large shared tiled screen space in order to accomplish their sensemaking tasks. Figure 2.14 shows both the arrangement of intelligence data and how the pair of analysts sat together when they worked on their issue.

A common need for most analysis tasks on large displays and multi-surface applications is the ability to visualize, manipulate, interact, and save the state of the work (or the state of the analysis) and to keep multiple states active in different forms. This allows analysts the ability to explore different directions and to reflect on the data while retaining the ability to return to previous directions. Large displays encourage collaboration, promote hypothesis testing and challenge each analyst to test their ideas with one another.

2.2.2   LARGE MULTI-TOUCH SURFACES AND COLLABORATION

Despite not yet being commonplace, large multi-touch surfaces have been available for a few years now, and some collaborative visualization systems have been developed specifically for them.

Figure 2.13: Teleboard display system. Creative designers collaborate over long distance using a mixture of touch and pen gestures on a projected whiteboard. Source: [74]

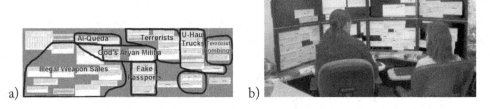

Figure 2.14: Large high resolution tiled display used for intelligence analysis. a) An overview of the layout of intelligence information on display. b) The look of the display. Source: [28]

In some cases, large surfaces have been used to enable collaboration generally; an example of this is uMeeting [124]. uMeeting uses a rear-projected multi-touch display to support co-located meetings using a software framework that allows shared documents to be accessed and manipulated (Figure 2.12). Large surfaces have also been used to support more specific collaborations, such as meetings of designers [74]. In each case, the larger surface area allowed for varying degrees of analysis using visualizations. In the design work example, designers used a vertical projector-based system called Teleboard (Figure 2.13) to share ideas and notes using touch, a digital pen, or even personal touch-based devices along with an electronic whiteboard as a means to share, visualize, or sketch ideas [74].

Displaying interactive visualizations on multi-touch surfaces allows analysts a whole new level of interaction. Data can be explored in parallel by multiple analysts. Data objects can be pushed, pulled, sorted, and visually arranged using natural gestures like those that would be used in exploring real-world objects. The digital form of the objects also enables annotation, highlighting, filtering, merging, and selecting. Gestures to zoom, pan and manipulate data ease exploration tasks. Example systems designed using this interaction paradigm began to appear early.

One such system is a touch surface designed to let analysts solve the VAST 2006 challenge [93]. Analysts work together on a touch enabled tabletop display which allows them to freely search, organize, and share documents. Through the use of touch-based gestures, documents can be zoomed and read in document readers, as well as repositioned and stacked on the surface. The end result is a system which gives analysts the ability to analyze and organize documents in a co-located setting (see Figure 2.15).

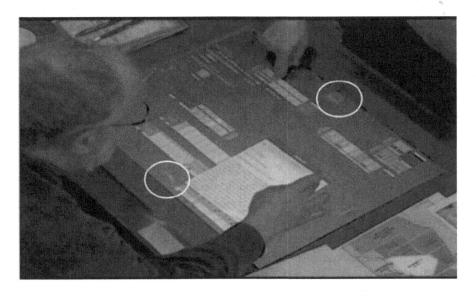

Figure 2.15: Touch-enabled tabletop to solve the 2006 VAST Challenge. Participants in the VAST challenge work together on a shared tabletop surface. Source: [93]

Recently, Kelleher and Grinstein partially implemented a multitouch system for exploring semantic graphs. They propose that small and large multi-touch displays are ideal for examining and navigating semantic graphs [105]. The graphs include a root node for the visualization, a scaling factor, and a panning vector. They suggest that the use of pinch for zoom and drag for panning makes exploration of this kind of data visualization very natural and should be further explored in future work on large touch displays.

Tobiasz and colleagues presented a system called Lark that supports co-located collaborative analysis on a shared multi-touch tabletop display [197]. The software presents visualizations of database information. The analysis process begins with a Raw Data Abstraction step, then an Analytical Abstraction step (pre-processing of the data such as scaling or filtering), then a Spatial Layout step (charting or graphing), and then finally a Presentation Level step (coloring aspects of charts and graphs). The system also leaves a trace of the analyst's steps, exposing different branches that have been explored. It supports parallel and joint work (See Figure 2.16) [197].

WebSurface, developed by Tuddenham et al., is a tabletop system designed to allow collaborative information gathering though web browsing [202]. The tabletop is designed so that two collaborators can work on the surface at the same time while easily managing their own data and passing data back and forth. Six front-mounted XGA projectors in a tiled display gives high resolution in order to ensure that text is readable at most sizes. The system supports the resizing, collecting and sharing of data. Figure 2.17 shows users collaboratively moving and interacting with documents on the display surface.

All these systems, while based on surface computing, principally leverage having a large interactive display. Other projects focus on other aspects of surface computing. For example, some systems look at the implications of using pens to interact.

One approach suggested is to use sketching as an interaction technique; this has been shown in a visualization system called SketchVis by Browne et al. [32] (See Figure 2.18 for an example sketch). The idea is to give analysts a way to both interact with and visualize real data using pen sketching techniques on a white board system. The system uses a digital pen as a method of input for drawing sketches and for all interactions with the system, such as drawing charts and graphs, labeling, and erasing. The benefit of this system is that it retains the simple stroke gesture that normally occurs when sketching, and thus supports the analysts' ability to quickly sketch out ideas and erase. Although the system does not use touch to interact with the visualizations, Browne et al. note that when it comes to resizing or manipulating charts and graphs and for erasure of sketches, a combination of touch and pen-based gestures is probably ideal. Despite the fact that the system is still in its early stages, the sketch-based interactions let analysts quickly explore data by using circling and strike-through pen gestures to modify the data that the charts show.

Another approach has been to explore the potential for interaction beyond the surface, where body gesture-based interfaces have been shown to be better for examining large volumetric data as compared with a traditional mouse.

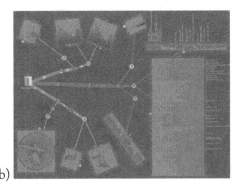

a)   b)

Figure 2.16: Multi-touch surfaces for analysis work. a) Student analysts jointly exploring information in a database by interacting with visualizations using touch gestures conveyed through a multi-touch table. b) An image of the tabletop display showing various visualizations and various paths in the analysis. Source: [197]

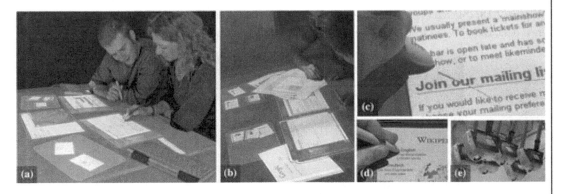

Figure 2.17: Websurface tabletop display. Users move and mark documents using styluses on the 6-projector high-resolution display. Source: [202]

Kirmizibayrak et al. studied the use of a 'magic lens,' which is a virtual circular area that is moved around in order to reveal underlying details, and the use of the Microsoft Kinect as a body gesture-based method of input to move the lens around [108]. In their study they found that although the mouse was more accurate for some tasks, such as specifying targets, the gesture-based interface was equal or better in terms of time to complete the tasks. They also found that the gesture-based interfaces were favored by users over mouse-based interfaces, and that in the context of medical practitioners examining large sets of volumetric data, gesture-based interfaces are beneficial when interacting with visualizations. The Kinect-based capture of gestures and the Magic Lens approach is shown in Figure 2.20.

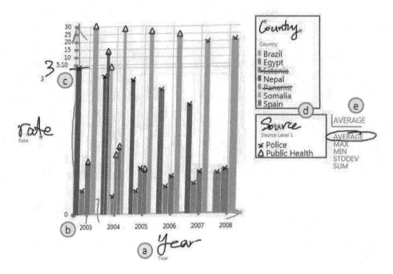

Figure 2.18: SketchVis: A sketch-based interactive system. By leveraging sketching techniques and real data, SketchVis allows quick generation and markup of data. Source: [32]

Figure 2.19: Tangible artifact used above the surface showing one possible interaction technique; still frame from demonstration video. Source: [188]

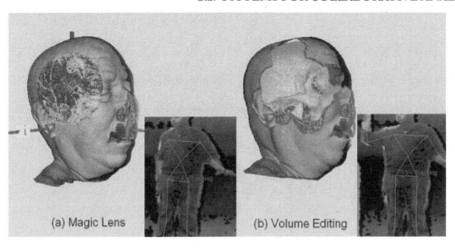

Figure 2.20: Magical Lens visualization and volume editing. Kinect-based gestures are used to rotate and move a Magic Lens to analyze medical data. Source: [108]

Spindler et al. also explore an approach to interacting with surfaces using tangible artifacts beyond the surface [187, 189]. In particular, they suggest some principles and how to apply them when designing the interaction with tangible artifacts. One example, taken from an online video demonstration, is shown in Figure 2.19 [188].

As a final example, we highlight the ideas of Dörk, Carpendale and Williamson and their tool called EdgeMaps analysis process [56]. The focus of their work was on the techniques for interaction, including arranging displays, panning, zooming, filtering, coloring, deleting, brushing, and linking. EdgeMaps depicts explicit and implicit relations within complex information spaces as shown in Figure 2.21. In this figure, the influence of the Beatles, and on the Beatles, is depicted in a similarity map of musicians using the multi-dimensional scaling technique to depict implicit relationships. Analysts can interact with the visualizations on large touch displays. They can zoom, expand, and look in detail. The main observation of the authors is that careful design of this interactivity encourages the user to become what they call an "information flaneur" (Flaneur was a term used by Baudelaire for someone who wanders the city in reflective exploration). The suggestion by Dörk, Carpendale and Williamson is that surface affordances can encourage the same kind of behavior, leading the user to develop a deep understanding of the domain represented by the system. This extends the work of Shneiderman, who decades earlier articulated the concept of direct manipulation, and presents possibilities addressed more fully in a paper by Lee et al. [119].

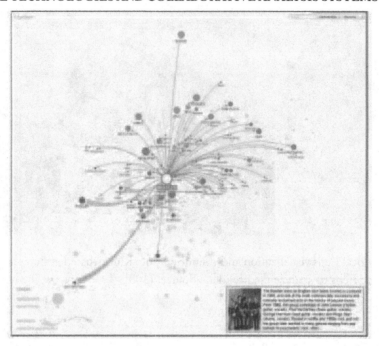

Figure 2.21: Edgemap visualizations for analysis work. The influence of the Beatles and on the Beatles depicted in a similarity map of musicians using the multidimensional scaling technique to depict implicit relationships. Source: [57]

2.2.3   MIXED-DISPLAY ENVIRONMENTS

A trend that has become important that relates to surface computing is the use of multiple devices in environments where different kinds of displays are used together, especially small mobile displays. We feel this approach is important for a pragmatic reason: many more display types are now affordable, and mobile devices have become ubiquitous. Moreover, this allows new opportunities: the ability for the displays to be oriented differently, and for mobile devices to be manipulated by individuals working as part of a group.

For example, Wigdor and colleagues designed WeSpace, a system of surfaces for co-located collaborative scientific analysis work [222]. Analysts bring laptops and link to a server. Images and movies on laptops can be shared on a large display, and manipulated indirectly through a tabletop that recognizes suitable touch gestures as shown in Figure 2.22. The system relies on screen sharing. It allows analysts to insert virtual pins on images and then link them together. This system of laptops, a wall display and a tabletop display, facilitates discussion and helps the team build associations between different parts of disparate data sets by pinning and linking items together as they talk.

Figure 2.22: WeSpace: A mixed-display environment for analysis work. An astrophysicists' meeting enabled by WeSpace. Source: [222]

Another example of the use of multiple devices along with a large display is Song et al.'s what-you-see-is-what-you-feel (WYSIWYF) system [186]. Small touch devices, such as the iPod Touch, are used in combination with a large display and various gestures to give the analyst a tool for interacting with visualizations of large sets of data. In their studies, Song et al. show that this method is very useful for analyzing 3D volumetric data along with annotating 3D slices. This combination of small devices with large devices gives analysts the freedom to view and manipulate large data locally while still retaining the visualization on the large display (Figure 2.23). The large display can also be manipulated with touch to allow rotation and translation of data. The system operates through the use of touch and tilt events sent by the iPhone SDK to a server PC which then uses those events to control, manipulate, or annotate the visualization.

A final example of a system that explores large data sets using multiple devices is the Slice WIM system, which enables analysts to explore complex 3D models using a touch table, along with a virtual reality environment [46]. The virtual environment is made possible through the use of a stereoscopic display wall, and slices of a 3D model projected onto a touch surface for analysis. Moving the 2D slice moves the corresponding 3D model and includes operations like rotation and translation using multi-touch gestures. Figure 2.24 shows a user examining a smaller virtual 3D model of blood flow in the SliceWIM interface. The head is tracked in order to maintain the stereoscopic view.

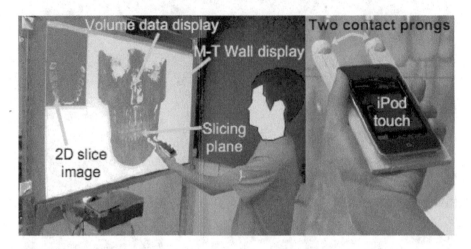

Figure 2.23: WYSIWYF interactive display. The combination of personal touch-enabled hand held devices such as the iPod touch allows analysts to interact with information on a larger display. Source: [186]

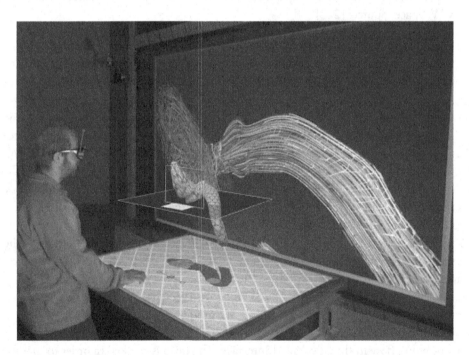

Figure 2.24: Slice World in Miniature (SliceWIM) VR interface. A user examines a high resolution simulation of blood flow in the VR environment. Source: [46]

2.3   ISSUES ARISING

We have outlined the main technologies of surface computing, and a set of systems relevant to collaborative data analysis.

The technology is still being explored and new approaches are being studied. However, there are now widely available devices. Small surfaces on smartphones and tablets have become ubiquitous, and support multi-finger interaction and gesture interaction using electronic touch-detection. Large surfaces, such as the Microsoft Surface and the SMART Table, also support multi-finger and gesture interaction, and sometimes fiducial marker recognition. They are not yet as widely distributed, but show great promise.

Systems designed for collaborative analysis typically leverage a large screen, and increasingly offer explicit support for collaborators. While such work began with conventional displays, the approach increasingly uses large surfaces to allow both viewing and interaction. As well as these basics, it appears that the interaction methods themselves, pointing and gesturing, offer advantages in this kind of environment. They signal to collaborators, as well as to the system, the intent of the interaction. Moreover, this mode of interaction may offer affordances that encourage exploration and reflection.

When considering such approaches, there are a variety of practical considerations to keep in mind. One is simply the cost and practicality of setting up multiple displays, such as the case with high resolution tiled displays, although these too are becoming more affordable. Another issue is that rooms should be large enough to accommodate the large displays, as well as to accommodate the users.

The lighting conditions for each style of display must be carefully considered when designing a shared space, as well as the mode of interaction. For example, as a gesture-based input, the Microsoft Kinect uses structured infrared light, which is significantly hampered by light from the sun and therefore should not be near windows. Similarly, projection-based displays must not have light interference which will mask or dilute the light coming from the projected surface. With respect to tiled displays, a very useful paper by Navràtil et al. outlines the significant requirements, including power specifications, rendering platforms, cost, performance, and recommendations [144].

In terms of software, very large displays often require multiple CPUs for rendering and computation, which in turn can cause applications to become coupled with their display mechanisms. Therefore, designers must be aware that in order to get the best performance out of their displays, such as when large visualizations of data are used, custom software, which takes full advantage of CPU and GPU resources, must be considered. In some cases performance boundaries may limit the visualization size and resolution that can be displayed.

Finally, there is a great need to develop task-specific software to realize the benefits of surface technologies. Such work is in its infancy, although there are a number of compelling examples, many of which have been reviewed in this chapter.

CHAPTER 3

Interacting with Surface Technologies

Buxton has emphasized that, at a minimum, the primary task of collaboration should not be impeded by technologies designed to support them [106]. Ideally, collaborative technologies should enable workflow.

Scott [179] was also concerned about workflow when she created the following guidelines for designing collaborative systems for tabletops. Her guidelines assert that technology should:

- support interpersonal interaction

- support fluid transitions between activities

- support transitions between personal and group work

- support transitions between tabletop collaboration and external work

- support the use of physical objects

- provide shared access to physical and digital objects

- consider the appropriate arrangements of users

- support simultaneous user actions

Workflow can be achieved through well-designed applications that support collaborative tasks, but workflow is also impacted by the minutiae of interactions with surfaces because these can distract from the primary purpose of collaboration. Therefore designing for collaborative tasks demands a lot of attention to the mechanisms of interaction because these have an enormous impact on flow. A vast amount of research has been directed toward enabling workflow by developing, testing and comparing interactive techniques. These are the primary challenges within the field at the moment because a gap remains between existing and ideal mechanisms for interaction.

Enabling workflow was the strongest argument made in Lee et al.'s recent paper on the importance of providing interactivity when working with visualizations [120]. Lee et al. claim that the information visualization community has made limited use of novel input devices and the field of human-computer interaction to advance the work of analysts. They argue that visualizations are an aid to making sense of data and to thinking, that interactions allow us to arrive at the right visualization that enables exploration and refinement of views and understanding, and that interaction is essential to enabling analytic discourse through which knowledge is constructed. Linking this to the topic of interaction design, the question then becomes, which interaction model is most effective? The authors draw us toward considering models that impose the least cognitive load on analysts, allowing more focus on analysis tasks and less on interface elements.

Moving away from the direct manipulation paradigm, which encompasses models like WIMP (windows, icons, mouse and pointer), instrumental interaction, and proxemic interaction, Lee et al. point to other broad paradigms as potentially more beneficial to analysts using visualizations including reality-based interfaces, surrogate interaction techniques and NUIs (natural user interfaces), all of which have been carefully defined in their article [120]. We pursue the latter model of interaction in this book, while also drawing on some good ideas from the direct manipulation paradigm. The NUI model of interface design for surfaces is described by Wigdor and Wixon and made possible by pen, touch, gesture, speech and sketching input mechanisms [223]. For very good descriptions of the other interface models, refer to Lee's paper [120].

Collaborative analysis work is not just about exploring or sharing visualizations, but can involve using raw data and many other types of information such as text, statistics, video, photos and maps. We feel that an exploration of the NUI model, that aims for an interface that is effectively invisible to its users and is based on nature or natural elements would help. It could direct design efforts toward creating interfaces for surface technologies that would allow analysts to manipulate digital artifacts on surfaces as they would manipulate tangible objects, i.e., in natural ways. We feel this would support collaborative analysis work across a broad spectrum of tasks.

This chapter looks closely at advances in some of the interaction mechanisms that tend to emphasize a more natural form of interaction and allow analysts to focus on the task at hand rather than on manipulating icons, menus, or instruments that are essential elements of other interaction models. In the language of Lee et al. [120], NUIs provide more 'degrees of freedom' so that there is a greater link between analyst intent and execution (i.e., exploration of data) which in turn enables workflow.

This section describes how the state of the art in interaction techniques for surface technologies is advancing.

3.1 POINTING AND SELECTING

Indexical communication involves pointing, which is ubiquitous in collaborative work. Sometimes pointing is used to draw the attention of others; however, sometimes pointing is a means of interacting with the system. When pointing on regular displays (with your cursor or finger), no interactive event is triggered. However, when using a touch display, an innocent indexical event can cause unintended system responses (e.g., pointing could be misinterpreted as a click by the system if the user touches the surface). In this subsection, we discuss this and other issues that relate to pointing and how pointing can be supported.

When interacting with large displays the question of reach often arises. Due to the physically large nature of the display, artifacts may be out of reach. Sometimes in a collaborative scenario, this problem might be solved by increased interaction between the collaborators (i.e., asking for something to be passed to you), which could lead to better shared awareness and better engagement, but sometimes this solution falls short or is simply not feasible. For example, imagine a 10-foot high, wall-sized display where no one can reach an artifact near the top of the screen. The ability to pan the screen could be useful for accessing out-of-reach artifacts, but this would disrupt other users working on different areas of the display. The solution to this problem is the subject of ongoing research that focuses on methods to extend a user's reach beyond their physical limits. We present a variety of solutions.

Shoemaker et al. used the embodiment of the user in the form of a translucent virtual shadow that is cast upon the surface using a virtual light source. This shadow follows the user's movements. The angle of the shadow can be adjusted to allow the user to interact with the interface using their shadow, without every having to actually touch the screen [183].

Banerjee introduces Pointable; users make in-air bi-manual gestures while wearing fiducial gloves. In this system the dominant hand controls the selection and movement of a remote object, while the other hand can execute tasks, such as rotating the object [12].

Marquardt et al. unified the space between surface gestures and mid-air gestures (also employing fiducial gloves), so that they can easily transition between direct-touch actions on displays and in-air movements. As part of this work, they introduced raycasting gestures, a technique that seamlessly integrates pointing above the table and direct-touch manipulation of a selected object. Used in the opposite sense, objects can be moved out of reach [130].

McAdam and Brewster designed an experiment to gauge the usability of interacting with a remote tabletop surface using a mobile phone [134]. They designed a system to test how well users could select and manipulate a dial and set it to a specified position. In one of three conditions the mobile phone duplicated the interface on the tabletop, and allowed the users to manipulate the tabletop interface indirectly using their phone. Their results were promising and they concluded that the phone as an input device for pointing and selecting had the best accuracy of all the techniques they studied.

A problem with pointing is that it is difficult to be precise. This problem regularly arises with applications designed for multi-touch surfaces. For high-resolution visualizations and analysis work, one could imagine that fingers could lack the necessary precision required for exploring data. In fact, they could hinder analysis work by obscuring information. Addressing the problem of 'fat fingers,' the disparity between object images on high resolution displays, and using fingers as a pointing device for selecting parts of an image, Voida and colleagues developed i-Loupe and iPodLoupe, which are lenses used on tabletop displays. These lenses (a rectangular green lens is shown in Figure 3.1) create a focus area where a magnified image of an object appears on a person's smartphone display, making it possible to select parts of it [211]. An alternative solution to the

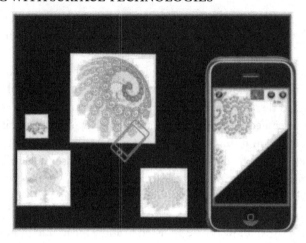

Figure 3.1: Selecting high resolution items with a low resolution pointing device. A solution to the 'fat fingers' problem encountered when using tabletop displays. A smartphone displays an enlarged image of a part of the tabletop display. The user selects a part of the image by touching the smartphone display. Source: [211]

precision problem for multi-touch systems would be a surface system that could also process input from multiple styluses.

Sometimes what the user wants to indicate is an area or a collection. This type of selecting is typically a prerequisite to another action, such as a move.

Bier et al. introduced the idea of using Toolglasses and Magic Lenses [22] for surface applications. These are transparent widgets that are dragged around the surface to reveal more detail about the objects underneath. This idea has been used to solve a variety of interaction issues including selection [5, 45, 171, 172].

In a similar vein, Appert introduced three techniques for focus + context lenses that combined the ability to zoom and precisely select small targets in the focus area [5]; and Kaser created FingerGlass [104], a bi-manual lens that allows precise selection within a zoomed area while maintaining the context of the focus area. Figure 3.2 illustrates how one hand activates the lens and maintains context while the other hand is free to interact with the area of interest.

Other solutions to selecting on a direct-touch device involve reducing problems of occlusion. Sometimes the objects users are trying to interact with are small and may be hidden completely or in part by fingers or hands which are in contact with the screen. If a single touch could trigger an enlarged view of the small items in a specialized area, then users could interact with those items there.

Figure 3.2: FingerGlass: A widget for interacting with large displays. The FingerGlass widget helps users see more detail and helps with precise selection. Source: [104]

3.2 GESTURING

Gestures introduce a novel method of interacting with touch-enabled surfaces. An understanding of designing gestures well is at the heart of the NUI interaction model and so we spend some time describing some useful taxonomies and theories that could be used to design gestures.

Wobbrock et al. identified form, nature, binding, and flow as dimensions in their taxonomy of surface gestures shown in Figure 3.3 [226].

The form of a gesture describes its shape at any point in time, and its path. If the shape of a gesture remains the same throughout movement over the display then it is static. If the shape changes then it is dynamic. The gesture is considered to have a path if there is movement other than simply changing the shape. For example, the dragging gesture shape is simply a finger blob; the gesture has a path because you move your hand across the screen, but while this happens the shape remains the same, it is always a finger blob. The pinching gesture's shape is dynamic because the two finger blobs are increasingly closer together, but the pinching gesture has no path because your hand does not move as you pinch.

The *nature* of a gesture is captured by four subcategories: symbolic, physical, metaphorical and abstract.

- Symbolic gestures are representations of things users can draw to trigger an action, such as drawing a question mark to activate help.

- Physical gestures are used to manipulate objects on the display.

- Metaphorical gestures are understood in terms of a user's mental model, and often the gesture represents an action. For example, walking your fingers across the screen could be the walking gesture in a game.

Taxonomy of Surface Gestures		
Form	static pose	Hand pose is held in one location.
	dynamic pose	Hand pose changes in one location.
	static pose and path	Hand pose is held as hand moves.
	dynamic pose and path	Hand pose changes as hand moves.
	one-point touch	Static pose with one finger.
	one-point path	Static pose & path with one finger.
Nature	symbolic	Gesture visually depicts a symbol.
	physical	Gesture acts physically on objects.
	metaphorical	Gesture indicates a metaphor.
	abstract	Gesture-referent mapping is arbitrary
Binding	object-centric	Location defined w.r.t. object features.
	world-dependent	Location defined w.r.t. world features.
	world-independent	Location can ignore world features.
	mixed dependencies	World-independent plus another.
Flow	discrete	Response occurs *after* the user acts.
	continuous	Response occurs *while* the user acts.

Figure 3.3: Wobbrock et al.'s taxonomy of surface gestures. Source: based on [226]

- Abstract gestures encapsulate all other gestures that do not fall into the three categories listed above. An example would be using a four finger tap to return to a starting point. Abstract gestures can be particularly difficult to design and they can be hard for users to learn and remember [103].

The *binding* dimension is primarily about the location of the gesture and its context or environment. This dimension of a gesture is categorized as: object-centric, world-dependant, world-independent and mixed.

- Object-centric gestures operate in a localized context, and they usually interact directly with or create objects. For example, the pinch gesture re-sizes an object to create a visualization of the same object only differently sized.

- World-dependent gestures are defined with respect to the real-world display environment. For example, dragging an object off-screen could move it into an imagined trash beside the screen in the real world.

- World-independent gestures require no information about the display environment, and generally can occur anywhere, except that the initial part of the gesture must not be performed on an object that can be manipulated by other gestures. A gesture to return to the desktop from any application is a good example.

- Mixed dependency gestures are simultaneously world-independent and either world-dependent or object-centric. A good example of this would be a rotation gesture where one finger from each hand is used. The first finger touches the desired object and acts as the point around which the object will rotate, while the other finger can be put anywhere else and is used to control the speed and rotation of the object.

The final dimension is *flow*. It describes a gesture in terms of what happens while it is being executed. A discrete gesture is one that must be executed entirely before anything happens on the display. An example would be a tap gesture to select an artifact, where the artifact is not selected until the gesture has completed. A gesture's flow is continuous if it requires constant recognition by the software. Continuous flow is required for the re-sizing gesture. As the user's fingers move closer together, the object becomes smaller, and as the user's fingers move further apart, the object gets bigger.

This taxonomy helps designers to understand the intricacies of gestures and can be used as an aid to software developers to structure gesture-recognition software. However, gesture design is far from a science and the above advice, directed toward designing a single gesture, is not clear enough to enable designers to easily associate a desired gesture with a suitable gesture type, nor does it provide guidelines for designing entire gesture sets.

Designing natural gestures is an open area where ongoing research is continuously producing new and better guidelines. Recently many papers have found value in involving both users and experienced designers in the design of new gestures [168, 226]. They have found that gestures designed using this user-centric technique produces gestures that are more natural and easier to remember.

A gestural interface for applications that support analysis work will necessarily have many abstract gestures to perform tasks where there is no adequate symbolic, physical or metaphoric representation. Examples of such tasks include, sorting, filtering, expressing a new hypothesis, and creating new paths of investigation. The design of gestures for these and other abstract concepts is even more challenging.

Hurtienne et al. introduced an important technique for designing abstract gestures that relies heavily on theories of cognition [89]. In their work they leverage the theory of image schemas and primary metaphors from cognitive psychology. Image schemas are knowledge about the world that is expected of a typical user. Everyone develops image schemas starting from their earliest interactions with the world as babies. Image schemas are developed based on experiences with the physical world, and they allow people to apply general concepts to multiple scenarios.

Up-down is an excellent example of an image schema. This is intuitively applied to many concepts like quantity or volume. For example, we understand without being told that as water is poured into a glass, the volume of water goes *up* or *increases*. Primary metaphors are the relationships between the image schema and the abstract concepts. When designing natural gestures,

Hurtienne advises leveraging these primary metaphors whenever possible to express abstract concepts within the application. For example, a gesture based on an up-down image schema could be created to *increase* or *decrease* the amount of information on the display.

3.3   HOVERING

Mouse-based systems provide different types of feedback and information about GUI elements when the user performs simple actions like placing the mouse pointer over top of a GUI element without clicking. Hover, or *linger* as it is sometimes referred to, is a specialized case of the mouseover or mouseout events that have existed since the first GUIs. At first these events were predominately triggered at the system level to change the appearance of the mouse cursor, thus cueing the user that further interaction was possible. Hovering has since been used to trigger tooltips or reveal information about an object. Today the use of hover is widespread and can be seen in all major operating systems from the Windows taskbar to the dock in Apple's OS X. Figures 3.4, 3.5, and 3.6 shows examples of how hovering is used in modern interfaces.

Figure 3.4: Hovering in web applications. A website designed for clickless mouse interaction that could be used for surfaces. Try it at: `dontclick.it`

GUI elements often listen for mouseover events and respond by divulging hidden opportunities to interact with the objects. This is a light-weight approach that encourages discovery and loose engagement so that users quickly learn to explore an interface without the need to commit to any particular action.

Modern webpages also leverage hovering as an interaction mechanism. The website `dontclick.it` was designed specifically for mouse interaction minus the clicks [97]. This system highlights the benefits of hovering for effortless exploration. Recent research has also addressed the importance of hovering to determine user's intents while they interact with web search results

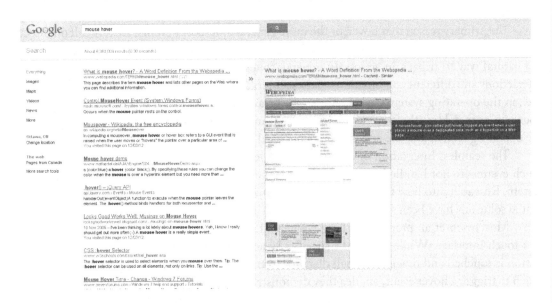

Figure 3.5: Hovering and Google Search. Hovering reveals a preview of search results. Source: www. Google.com

Figure 3.6: Hovering in Windows. Lingering the mouse pointer on top of the folder icon in a Windows taskbar to reveal a quick preview of open folders.

[88]. This principle was applied by designers of Google's search engine so that hovering to the right of any search result item now reveals a preview of that result without requiring a visit to a web page.

The primary reason that hover, or the more general mouseover events, are difficult on direct-touch, mouseless systems is that direct touch requires physical contact with the surface, and this is a natural way to trigger an action. In general, touch-based systems recognize several types of interactions and different combinations of these interactions, but at the lowest level of the software (i.e., in the operating system), what this is often translated to is 'touch down,' 'touch move' and 'touch up' events. How these events are interpreted and combined is dependent on the framework, the operating system and the application being used.

The seamless integration of touch and the operating system is still a work in progress and touch events are not handled in a consistent manner between systems or even within the same system. Research into how to port hover to direct-touch environments is ongoing and many potential solutions have been suggested.

Moscovich et al. proposed sliding widgets [138] as a replacement for traditional buttons in a touch interface. While they don't specifically address hovering, their design requires that a button is touched and dragged a small distance to trigger a 'click.' This therefore leaves a simple touch to trigger a hover event, an idea they demonstrated as workable in a word processor where a simple touch on an alignment button invoked an alignment preview. If the user then dragged the button slightly, the alignment setting was applied (and the button popped back into its original place). This solution helps avoid accidental activation and incorrect selection, which can be caused by the difficulties of precise selection on touch surfaces.

Using Bier et al.'s Toolglass and Magic Lenses technique for selection, it is also possible to design a hover lens that would trigger a preview of a target object. Dragging the widget above an object would trigger the hover event, just as if the mouse cursor had been placed above the object.

Another method for enabling hovering was proposed by Benko et al. who suggested that pressure could be used to differentiate between a hover and a click [16]. In this research, pressure-sensitive devices were used to trigger a hover event based on the amount of force used when touching the screen. They simulated a pressure sensitive display with SimPress, where a rocking motion on a target object with a finger activates a listening state in a widget. Once activated, the system computes the touch area of the finger. A smaller area triggers a hover event, while a larger area triggers a click event, as shown in Figure 3.7.

Other solutions suggest the use of cameras to detect interaction above or in front of the surface. In this case, depth-sensing algorithms can detect an approaching finger or pen [225]. Pyryeskin developed a technique for vision-based multi-touch tables where they leveraged additional information that cameras typically provide, other than the blobs that correspond to touches. This allowed them to detect several layers of hover space above the table [159].

Figure 3.7: A solution to hovering on large displays. On the left a smaller finger blob represents a lighter touch and triggers a hover action. The right side shows a larger finger blob which in dictates a more forceful touch and triggers a click action. (The top left image in both sides show the shape of the blob detected by their system.) Source: [16]

3.4 TEXT

The ability for collaborators to simultaneously enter text while working around a large shared display is important for the efficiency of their workflow. In many scenarios the use of multiple physical keyboards is impractical for a few reasons. On a large horizontal display there is usually no good place to put the physical keyboards—they would potentially take up too much space and could occlude artifacts from view if they were placed on top of the surface. Similarly, on vertical wall-mounted displays, the question of where to put keyboards still exists. Currently there are two dominant areas of investigation to provide alternative solutions to physical keyboards, and both involve the use of virtual or soft keyboards.

One approach is the use of virtual keyboards designed for use on large interactive surfaces. Another is to investigate the use of mobile devices like smartphones and tablets which have their own virtual keyboards. They can be used for text entry in a more familiar way, since the use of virtual keyboards on handheld devices is increasingly common, while large interactive displays are only starting to make their way into real work environments.

Ko et al. investigated the size of the virtual keyboard, and whether or not the keyboards used on smartphones could be used equally well when ported to large surfaces [111]. They studied the usability of virtual keyboards in terms of speed and accuracy, but also considered space (how much screen real estate is used to display the virtual keyboard), occlusion (the effects of the user's fingers occluding the actual keys) and robustness (the tolerance for calibration errors as a result of older, lower resolution displays). The results of the study showed that the best performing keyboard was a more traditional QWERTY keyboard as seen in Figure 3.8. They also found that methods developed for mobile devices to help with the occlusion of the keys had little impact on the larger displays, even when the virtual keyboards were quite small compared to the screen.

Gesture Keyboard was introduced as a low cost prototype developed by Murase et al. [142]. With this system any built-in display camera or webcam can be used to detect typing on the

Figure 3.8: A simple QWERTY virtual keyboard. Source: [111]

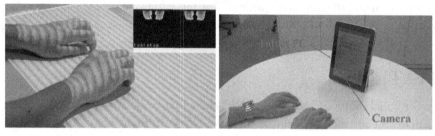

(a) Anywhere Touchtyping   (b) Gesture Keyboard

Figure 3.9: Text input on large displays. a) Anywhere touch typing uses an overhead DPL projector and high-speed camera to detect typing on a surface. Source: [140] b) Gesture Keyboard, a simple invisible keyboard, uses the built in camera or webcam to detect typing. Source: [142]

surface in front of the display. Anywhere Touchtyping is another low cost alternative and was developed by Mujibiya et al. [140]; it uses an overhead DPL projector in combination with high speed video capture camera to detect typing on surfaces in front of a display using depth sensing algorithms. Figure 3.9 shows an example of both of these techniques.

3.5   IDENTITY OF THE INTERACTOR

Often it can be useful for the application to be aware of its users' identities. This knowledge can be leveraged for access control of shared or personal artifacts, the activation of personal or private work areas, or to better understand the potentially complex interactions of multi-touch and multi-user gestural interfaces. To clarify the latter point, imagine two users who are simultaneously interacting with a gestural-based interface. If each touch can be traced back to a particular user then the system's gestural recognition engine will be less likely to confuse the actions of separate users as a single gesture, and therefore it will be able to correctly identify gestures that are performed simultaneously by multiple users.

Recent work by Marquardt et al. developed the TouchID Toolkit, which was designed to facilitate the rapid development of touch aware applications through an event driven API [131]. It used fiduciary gloves to provide the system with user identity as well as hand or finger orientation and traditional touch and gesture recognition. In this system, each fiduciary tag on the glove could be assigned to specific tasks allowing quick access to a number of customizable tasks.

Schmidt introduced IdLenses [171], a widget that is invoked when a user places their hands down on the surface. It incorporated previous work called HandsDown [170], which was a system able to recognize a registered user based on the contour of their hand. Once a user is recognized, a re-sizable lens is used to create a private work area on the shared surface. Figure 3.10 shows a few uses of this novel lens. Information can be automatically entered in fields based on the user's id. Comments can be seamlessly identified with their authors.

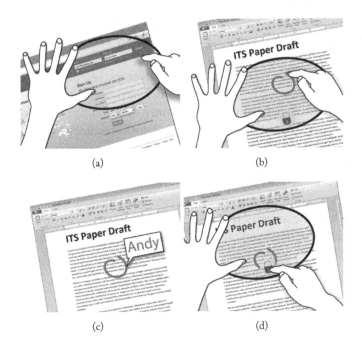

Figure 3.10: A few examples of how IdLenses can be used. a) Dragging the lens above a login screen allows automatic entry of login credentials. b) Annotation of documents. c) An example of how the annotation looks when other users are viewing the document. d) Private annotations that are invisible to others can be made by drawing the annotation through the lock button. Source: [171]

Sometimes hardware can provide partial solutions to the identity problem. The Diamond-Touch table by Circle Twelve Inc. is a multi-user, touch- and gesture-activated surface that supports small group collaboration. An array of antennas embedded in the touch surface works in conjunction with a receiver that is connected to individual users (typically through their chair) to allow the table to distinguish between the touches of the various collaborators. This has significant benefits for avoiding misunderstandings by the software when many hands are on the display at once. Gestures can be interpreted easily if the system knows which multi-touches correspond with each other.

Pen-based systems like Anoto also aid with distinguishing between collaborators because each collaborator can have their own Anoto pen.

3.6   ISSUES ARISING

Interaction issues that are particularly important to analysis work include the following:

Individual work with digital artifacts using laptop and workstation computers in theory should be more compatible with digital tabletops and digital wall displays, since digital artifacts don't have to be transformed into analog (paper) artifacts to be taken to a meeting. In practice, however, the problem of moving digital artifacts seamlessly between surfaces has not yet been resolved.

Human communication is rife with indexical references, i.e., pointing, which involves verbally or physically indicating something. In artifact-rich environments pointing behavior is common and saves much time. Anecdotally it is well known that pointing, which is so easy on a singular small display with a mouse input controlling a cursor, becomes much more difficult when more displays are added, displays are tiled, or when the display becomes much larger.

There is still much to be learned about how to leverage the new dynamics of a multi-input, multi-user system and many interaction issues still need to be addressed. For example, pointing, selecting, gesturing, hovering, text input and interactor identity are all currently the subject of active research. Once the answers emerge, efforts will be necessary in the development and compliance of standards for touch interaction.

CHAPTER 4

Collaborative Work Enabled by Surfaces

4.1 COLLABORATION

We begin by defining what we mean by *collaboration,* a remarkably vague term [73]. Working at the inter-organizational level, Mattessich, Murray-Close and Monsey made distinctions between collaboration, cooperation and coordination based largely on the intensity of *inter-agency* interactions [132].

Concerning *intra-agency* small-group tasks, McGrath has emphasized differences between group tasks that embody cooperation versus 'conflict' [135], which he and Straus later reconceptualized as low versus high interdependence [190]. In this book we primarily address intra-agency collaboration. However, in either exploration of the definition, we feel there is a spectrum being explored, but also a clear understanding that not every interaction or group activity is considered to be collaborative. In general, group activities that can be described as *collaborative* tend to be more intense and have greater interdependence between team members, which arises from the fact that the collaborative group is jointly committed to achieving a common goal.

In the context of intra-agency collaboration, Okada has conceptualized this spectrum as a hierarchy of different types of groups. Collaborative groups are at the top (greatest interdependence), below groups that share resources, groups that exhibit awareness, and groups where individuals coexist with one another [150]. Denise has also proposed a hierarchy of group activities, also with collaborative groups at the top [53] for the same reason as Okada.

Some work, focusing on types of collaborative activity (intense and goal-focused), has explored collaboration from the perspective of its 'modes' or 'phases.' From this perspective collaborative activity, or a collaborative project, can be broken down into commonly occuring phases. For example, Grudin and Poltrock describe three phases that can occur in any collaborative activity: communication (dialoguing), information sharing, and coordinating (project management) [73]. Various tools support the various phases, e.g., chat supports group communication or dialoguing. Similarly, Herskovic et al. describe three technology-mediated phases of collaboration: communication, coordination and cooperation (actual joint work on a shared task) [49]. We find additional value in a lesser known model of the phases of collaboration that puts an emphasis on a phase of interacting that happens in teamwork when groups transform their practices [64]. From the perspective of Engeström's research, collaboration includes these three phases: coordination (coordinated work), cooperation (joint work), and reflective communication (work that reflects on the team's process with an eye to improving it). This model suggests that this transformation occurs when groups reflect on, i.e., talk about, their activity. When people *reflectively communicate* they "reconceptualize their own organization and interaction in relation to their shared objectives" [64]. This occurs when tensions build and work as normal must be re-evaluated and developed, for example, to re-assess objectives or tweak practices, or to introduce new roles.

Perspectives that highlight the various phases of collaborative work are useful because they more clearly specify the purposes surfaces may serve. There are clearly a range of models that can be leveraged. Most researchers, many of whom have developed collaborative tools, have focused on only one of these aspects, such as Olson, Malone and Smith whose research has focused on the coordination aspects of collaborative work (i.e., how to help team members interleave their work with others) [151].

Another important aspect when considering the range of activities that are collaborative is the space and time continua within which collaborations occur, as this is an important issue when designing software for groups [73]. Collaboration may involve homogeneous or non-homogeneous groups who may or may not be co-located or working synchronously. We emphasize co-located analysis teams who are working synchronously around tabletops or large displays.

Examining types of group activities, McGrath's research resulted in a very general taxonomy. He identified 8 types: planning, creativity, intellective (solving problems with correct answers), decision-making (deciding issues with no right answer), cognitive conflict (resolving conflicts of viewpoints), mixed motive (resolving conflicts of interest), competitive (resolving conflicts of power) and performance-based [135]. As mentioned in the introduction, the types of primary relevance to *collaborative analysis work* are intellective tasks, and decision-making, both of which are judgment tasks characterized as 'choosing' processes that require group members to work interdependently [190].

An extensive literature exists on collaboration, and many general results have been reached concerning collaborating teams. Results show that, on average, groups perform better than the average of their members, or than a randomly selected member, although not necessarily better than their best member. The better overall result is explained by the group's aggregate skills and by synergy (the building up of good ideas) [114]. Synergy is especially a positive factor in multidisciplinary teams, so collaborative work by multi-skilled teams has many advantages.

However, researchers have also found that the performance of the group depends to a very large extent on conditions, such as the type of task they are given, the nature of the institution in which they are operating, the individual's interpretations of their conditions and institution, available tools, and the skillsets of team members [114, 157]. Many studies have also shown there is a great deal of variance in *how* groups collaborate even when many factors are the same. This result has also been verified in the analysis domain where groups of analysts collaborating around a tabletop adopted many different strategies when solving the VAST 2006 Challenge, which was a 'sensemaking' task involving a corpus of 280 documents [93]. These results suggest that understanding the factors that contribute to a positive collaborative outcome in any given situation, including collaborative analysis, is complex. In this chapter we focus on one particular aspect, the displays and surfaces that may be used by collaborating analysts.

Barriers to research on collaborative analysis include the requirement for authentic and challenging problems, the reality of dealing with large data sets, the complexity of data gathering and analysis techniques, difficulties engaging experienced analysts as participants in studies, and barriers to conducting field studies (especially if the material being analyzed is sensitive). However, despite these significant challenges, researchers are developing standardized problem sets that are large enough to be interesting, and are finding ways to bring analysts into labs to study their behavior under more controlled conditions, such as various arrangements of surfaces.

4.2   DESIGN OF RESEARCH ON COLLABORATION AND DISPLAY TECHNOLOGIES

In this section we review experimental research on the benefits of additional display space for individuals and teams, especially with respect to intellective and sensemaking tasks. Reviewing the benefits of additional display space for individual work is important because many of these are carried over into collaborative situations. We then discuss the pros and cons of using surface technologies for collaborative work. Throughout we emphasize the importance of good design. We conclude the chapter by reviewing several case studies of organizations that have adopted surface technologies to enable collaborative work.

One of the difficulties in reviewing this research has been making sense of results that are sometimes about display size width and length or diagonal span (measured in inches), and sometimes about pixel dimension or what many authors call 'resolution' (measured in megapixels). Pixel density (measured in dots per inch or, more properly, pixels per inch) is rarely mentioned. Pixel (or dot) density is a function of the the display 'resolution' and the size of the display, and a better indicator of true resolution. Some confusion occurs because a larger display does not necessarily imply a greater or even equivalent pixel density. Most authors assume readers will have intuitive insight into pixel density knowing the diagonal measure of the display and the display resolution measured in megapixels. When reading papers, it's useful to notice whether or not the pixel density remains constant or increases with the display size. This can be a little tricky to assess, since the calculations for pixel density require the length and width of the screen and not the diagonal measurement. Other display specifications, such as contrast ratio, refresh rate, and total luminance, also exist, but to this point these have not been studied very much.

Experiences with displays can also be explored through an understanding of human perceptual abilities. Visual acuity, which is the ability of a user to distinguish a pixel, is sometimes discussed. For example, it is known that at very high pixel densities individual pixels cannot be distinguished. This implies that at some point a pixel density can be reached beyond which further increases cannot be perceived. Another perceptual issue to be aware of is visual field. The distance of the viewer from a display can have an impact on visual field, which is a relevant consideration for larger displays. Other perceptual abilities could also be explored, but as this brief discussion shows, it's wise to concurrently consider both the technical specifications of displays and human perceptual abilities at the same time.

A third issue is individual variation in vision and perception. For example, visual accuity varies between individuals and also as a function of eye-to-screen distance, especially for older viewers who may have bifocal or progressive glasses. Additionally, some individuals are color blind.

Researchers are also interested in the varying impact that changing display sizes, resolutions, and configurations can have on users. They have studied the impact on efficiency, satisfaction, memory mechanisms and so on. In terms of displays and output measures, the variations are considerable. For an excellent and nuanced discussion of large-format displays and the topics of display availability, display size, tiling, resolution, human perception and research with these types of displays, see Moreland's recent paper [136].

With many gaps in the literature and technology advancing rapidly, there is much potential for research in this area. Here we try to review research with an eye to understanding the impact of technical variations in the context of individual and collaborative analysis work. Analysis work, for example, may benefit to a certain extent from a wider visual field (e.g., when data is overlaid on maps), which may make it easier to build cognitive maps. Alternately, a greater pixel density for some types of visualizations may improve performance on spatial tasks [232]. Research into these areas is active and ongoing.

4.3   LARGE DISPLAYS AND INDIVIDUAL ANALYSIS WORK

In this section we review the literature on the many advantages of additional monitors or larger displays for individuals in typical workplaces.

4.3.1   GREATER SATISFACTION, AWARENESS & EFFICIENCY, DECREASED COGNITIVE LOAD

An individual given the opportunity to have multiple 17" or 19" monitors will use the additional space wisely. After observing and interviewing 18 software workers, Grudin found that the benefits of multiple displays over single displays in their workspace included using the additional space for peripheral awareness tasks (such as the arrival of new emails), which keeps individuals connected to external events, and for 'parking' resources that might be useful in the near future, an act which reduces cognitive load by eliminating a search task. Overall he found that the net result of multiple displays was improved efficiency, even though the applications individuals were using were not designed to take advantage of multiple monitors. [72].

Morris and colleagues manipulated the workplace environment to study how individuals would make use of additional displays [137]. They moved an additional display that was sensitive to stylus input into the work environment of eight office workers with diverse jobs and watched how they used that additional display in addition to their own 20"- 21" 1600 x 1200 (1.9 megapixels) PC display or their own dual PC displays. For the first two weeks they positioned the additional display (also 1.9 megapixels) vertically, and for the next two weeks they positioned it

Figure 4.1: Testing the benefits of additional displays. Images a) and d) show two types of typical office environments: one display or two displays respectively. Images b) and e) show an additional vertical display inserted into the two types of environments. Images e) and f) show an additional horizontal display inserted into the two types of environments. Source: [137]

horizontally (See Figure 4.1). The researchers found that an interactive *horizontal display* was *not* a useful addition to a knowledge worker's office (they thought it might have proved a useful aid for note taking or sketching). They also found that participants used displays differently based on their orientation, and that individuals had orientation preferences. They suggested many design improvements to make using multiple displays easier. At the end of their study they concluded knowledge workers can make use of up to at least triple the regular display space, even though interface issues, such as navigating between screens with a mouse, presented challenges. We next consider other outcomes of providing individuals with larger displays.

4.3.2 INCREASED PRODUCTIVITY; AN AID TO MEMORY

Czerwinski et al. wondered if a typical office worker would be more productive with the large (12" x 42"), horizontal, 3072 x 768 (2.3 megapixals), curved display shown in Figure 4.2 in comparison to a single smaller 15" display of unstated, but presumably, standard pixel dimensions [50, 164]. Fifteen individuals tried out these two display arrangements in a lab study with realistic cognitively-loaded office-worker tasks that required a lot of task switching and that used typical Microsoft Office products. For these types of tasks, and despite the fact that the operating system had not been designed for large displays, the researchers found the large display had a significant (i.e., their results were not by chance) 9% productivity advantage over a single smaller display.

Figure 4.2: Benefits of large displays. This large display was preferred by study participants and was also rated more satisfying than a regular-sized display Source: [50, 164]

Ball and North explored the benefits of a 37" x 44", 3840 x 3072 (11.7 megapixels) 3x3 tiled display, which was comprised of nine monitors, each of which were larger and had greater resolution than typical displays. They wondered about the impact of increasing the quantity and granularity of displayed information. For six months they studied the ad hoc use of this large display (shown in Figure 4.3) and then for three months they studied five people in typical business environments using the display in a time-sharing manner. The advantages they found were "improved user performance for task switching or viewing large documents, increased ability to spatially position applications and shortcuts for quick access and recall, bezel adaptations for easy separation of tasks, increased ability to work collaboratively, increased screen space for awareness of secondary tasks and increased enjoyment" [10]. Their more extensive longitudinal study began to point to other benefits of large displays. They found that the positive experience with the tiled display reported by their participants increased over time. Also, large displays appeared to enable paired collaborative work.

Other research has more carefully qualified the benefits, emphasizing the importance of good design more strongly, or highlighting some limitations of early positive results. Tan, Stefanucci, Proffitt and Pausch studied the impact of using three monitors and two projection displays (which provided a total viewing angle of 145 degrees) with respect to their function as potential memory aids. They concluded that large displays *can* be an aid to human memory *if* they are well designed to provide users with contextual cues [194]. Similarly, early studies that showed performance increases with larger displays at proportionally higher pixel dimensions [11, 184] have been superseded by studies that show there may be application-specific limits on the "larger is better" principle. Jakobsen and Hornbaek used six 24" LCD monitors and tested performance with either all, 1/9th or 1/81st of the available space. They found their medium-sized display space of 1.5 megapixels was as effective as a larger, higher-resolution display space of 13.8 megapixels for certain mouse-based navigation tasks with maps [100].

Figure 4.3: Benefits of high-resolution tiled displays. This tiled display was used for a variety of tasks by five participants over three months. Typically participants used the central display for the home page and surrounding displays for additional documents and spreadsheet data. Source: [10]

Many of the previous studies could not provide explanations for their results. Other studies interested in explaining *why* more display space has benefits have shown there are decreases in cognitive load due to a reduction in the time spent switching between tasks and less time spent navigating [72, 193]. A study by Andrews, Endert and North showed *how* analysts used a 4x2 array of 30" LCD monitors, i.e., a 2560 x 1600 (32 megapixels) tiled display space (shown in Figure 4.4) in creative and individualistic ways. When they compared student analysts using either a typical 17" monitor or the array of high-resolution monitors they found no differences in the time to complete an analysis task or the completeness of the analysis, but found substantial behavioral differences. They concluded the six larger displays played an important role as external memory for the analyst, as evidenced by the fact the analysts with the 17" monitor required more external aids (paper notes and compilation documents) to complete tasks. In a second lab study with real analysts, Andrews et al. showed how the larger display was an aid to organizing work, which was valuable for evidence marshaling and schematizing [4]. Analysts in this second study created clusters of potentially interesting documents, background documents, critical documents, etc., as a way of immersing themselves into their data corpus.

4.3.3   LARGE DISPLAYS AND LARGE VISUALIZATIONS

In the domain of visualizations for analytics, there are careful design issues to consider when contemplating the use of very large displays. What would happened if visualizations could simply spread out on very large, very high resolution displays so everything could be seen at once, eliminating the need to design visualizations of data aggregates, to design functions to eliminate unnecessary data, or to design navigation techniques to explore the data? Yost and North dis-

Figure 4.4: Benefits of large displays for organizing the analysis task. An analyst at work with his 32 megapixel workstation. Source: [4]

covered that it depends somewhat on both the visualization type and the characteristics of the display. Varying both, they found that graphical encodings to indicate differences in data types are more important on a smaller display (two 17" 2M displays in a 1 x 2 array) with less data (252 data points), while spatial groupings of data of similar type are more important on a larger display (twenty-four 17" 32MP displays in a 3x8 array) with more data (5488 data points) [231]. These results suggest that simply spreading visualizations out over a larger space is not the best approach because design guidelines change for larger displays.

In a more extreme study, Yost and North wondered what would happen to attribute-centric and space-centric visualizations if displays varied in pixel density above, at or below resolutions at which a person at a certain distance was able to distinguish two pixels on a display. They used the same very large display array (twenty-four 17" 32MP displays in a 3x8 array) to create visualizations of large maps with embedded graphs and charts (see Figure 4.5) [232]. Depending on the experimental condition, they employed some or all of this large display to test the impact of larger visualizations to below, at, or above the level of visual acuity. To complicate interpretations, but as a matter of necessity, more data was displayed on larger displays. The visualizations were either 5,488, 23,548 or 94,192 data points, with the middle condition matching the visual acuity of humans. In general they found performance on most tasks was more efficient and sometimes more accurate "when showing more data using larger displays" because of the additional data that could be displayed, and despite the requirement for physical navigation required on the larger displays. They concluded that information visualizations could be usefully scaled up to very large displays. The detailed results showed that there were differences between visualization types with space-centric visualizations (e.g., maps with embedded data) seeming to be more able to scale

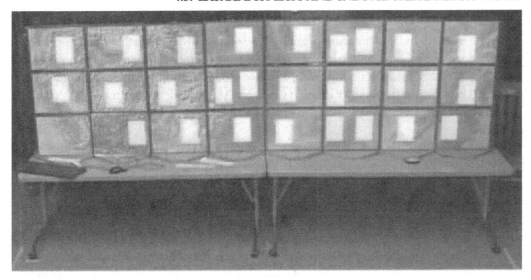

Figure 4.5: Benefits of large displays for map data. This very large 24-monitor high-resolution display displayed 21 times the information of a 2-monitor display condition. Although it was physically demanding, individuals were able to perform many information seeking tasks on these large displays. The display showed a topological map of the United States with tables placed at appropriate locations. Source: [232]

up to the the largest size (beyond visual acuity) while simultaneously remaining useful, while attribute-centric visualizations were less able to scale up beyond visual acuity and remain useful.

In Yost and North's study, navigation of visualizations was 'physical,' which meant users walked along the display front looking for data, and interacting with the data was not a possibility. More recently, a study that addressed *interacting* with maps with a mouse using standard navigation techniques over varying display sizes (but none that required physical navigation), found that results depended strongly on the navigation task being performed, but that in general, navigation on small displays (.17 MP) was hardest. Navigation on very large displays (six 24" 1920x1200 LCD monitors arranged in a 3x2 grid providing 13.8 MP) and medium sized displays (1.5 MP) were largely comparable, with an 'overview plus detail' navigation mechanism performing best relative to those tried, even though with very large displays there were more mouse movements and longer search times. [100]. When scaling a visualization up to display it on a larger size display these results suggest that navigation techniques may have to switch from one type to another.

4.3.4 IMPLICATIONS FOR COLLABORATION

The overall results for individuals using larger high-resolution displays are that these displays have a variety of cognitive benefits, aiding memory and reducing cognitive load in many ways. Research has also shown that individuals rapidly make effective use of additional display space and enjoy it. This result is also true in the security domain where analysts may be awash in a sea of documents and where large displays have the potential to help analysts effectively and creatively organize their work.

However, results also indicate that the total amount of display space an individual can effectively make use of and enjoy is not unlimited, with studies suggesting somewhere been four to eight typically sized monitors is maximal. Issues to be aware of include human visual resolution acuity, peripheral vision acuity, and so on, which we have addressed only briefly. Other issues include the challenges of navigating larger display spaces, especially when the input device is a mouse that crosses display boundaries awkwardly.

Some results are mixed, especially when it comes to evaluating different tasks (such as navigation tasks) because some tasks are performed better on some display arrangements in comparison to others, and particular results may depend on the design of the study and may not generalize to every domain. However, most researchers have concluded that designing for larger displays with higher resolutions is not the same as designing for standard display sizes.

In summary, the research on adding additional display space for individual workers is very positive, especially for tasks that require many analytic artifacts or documents. We reviewed this work because many of the advantages carry over to collaborative surfaces where individuals are also working with large displays and one would expect benefits like increased satisfaction with the large display space, decreased cognitive load due to digital artifacts being simultaneously visible and so on, to be the same. Also, work conducted in isolation is brought to collaborative encounters so large displays in individual workspaces can have an indirect impact on collaborative work. At this time, the evidence for large visualizations is less compelling, with early results showing that large maps can be effectively displayed and used on large displays, though navigation techniques should be designed differently for differing display sizes.

4.4 SURFACES AND TEAM COLLABORATIONS

A major difference between the research on individuals and larger displays in comparison to groups and large displays or surfaces is that research on groups is more concerned about how the group as a whole functions. This means different impacting factors, such as group awareness and team performance become important. Another difference is that there is a decrease in interest in display size or pixel dimension and more interest in the impact of varying the input style. In this section, we consider the research on the value of larger and proportionately higher-resolution displays for supporting *collaborative* work. Most of this research is fairly recent, but a picture of the benefits is emerging nevertheless.

4.4.1   INCREASED AWARENESS AND PERFORMANCE

Collaborative tasks are joint endeavors. A shared display can be used to support increased awareness of team member actions, to display changes in the work situation, and to post information important to the team. Improved situation awareness enables seamless collaboration allowing people to move between individual and shared activities, provides a context in which to interpret communication, aids in anticipating the actions of others, and reduces the effort to coordinate tasks and resources [76]. In many mixed-focus and partially distributed, mission-oriented collaborative tasks involving analysis of disparate information, increased awareness can be especially important because real-time information from the field is often needed by centralized decision-makers. Providing situation awareness aids using displays or surfaces helps because team work will flow more easily because talk within the team will not have to be about team actions, changes in the work situation, and so on.

Bolstad and Endsley are pioneers in the area of situation awareness for collaborative work. Through experimental research they found that situation awareness can be enhanced by the development of shared displays that have been purposefully designed to make visible the critical information of relevance to decision-making teams. Their results show that the value of shared displays increases with the workload level, and that displaying information that enhances situation awareness leads to an improvement in performance in team tasks [24, 25]. These are important gains directly applicable to collaborative analysis work.

From their understanding of the value of situation awareness with respect to performance, Riley, Bolstad and Endsley studied military situations where there was a need to perceive, interpret and exchange large amounts of frequently ambiguous information to maintain the situation awareness necessary for effective decision-making during missions. To design an awareness system for a regular display that would support effective decision-making during military missions, the researchers conducted 'goal-directed task analysis' interviews with 20 subject-matter experts that focused on the shared goals and shared information needs of collaborators [163]. They found that large amounts of frequently ambiguous information was needed to maintain situation awareness. This knowledge helped the researchers to develop an application for a shared display to enable situation awareness. Their screen design, shown in Figure 4.6, considered many aspects of the decision-making context, including balancing individual and team situation awareness needs, making assumptions about roles and procedures clear, and enabling the creation of action plans and contingency plans. Their work provided a generic process for designing displays to enhance situation awareness that would be applicable across varying interface styles.

One study of tabletop users compared the impact of input devices on situation awareness. In their study, Hornecker, Marshall, Dalton and Rogers compared (indirect) mouse input and (direct) touch input to investigate the importance of surface attributes. They asked 13 groups of three people to work on a real planning task that involved assigning individuals to locations in a new building that was being designed at the time for the people who were in the study. They analyzed videos of the groups at work and compared negative and positive awareness behaviors as

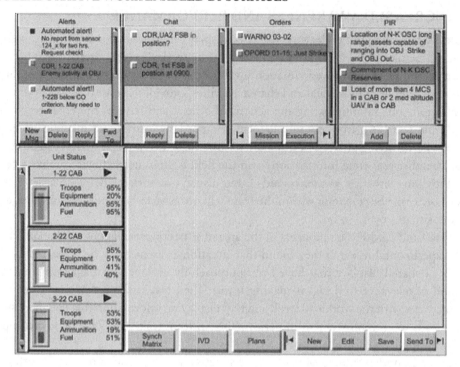

Figure 4.6: Designing to support situation awareness when rapid decisions must be made. A display to enable 'global' situation awareness of various team members in a military situation. The information displayed aligns with the capabilities and needs of a specific team role. The display above was designed for a regular-sized display for operations personnel. Different displays were designed for intelligence and logisitcs personnel. Each team member uses multiple displays, and in general knows only what is useful to them about the activities of others on the team. Source: [163]

well as noting 'awareness work.' In favor of surfaces, the multi-touch condition resulted in higher awareness. Their overall conclusion supported the use of multi-touch tabletop interfaces over mouse-driven tabletop systems for enhancing situation awareness [86]. Using the more direct multi-touch input and interacting around the tabletop surfaces apparently kept the team more closely aligned.

Inkpen, Mandryk and Whalen also drew attention to the importance of selecting the right input device when designing tabletop systems to enhance the awareness of another person's intentions. They found that direct input devices, such as touch and stylus, increased awareness of the intentions of other team members working at a tabletop and indirect input devices, such as mice, provided less support for increased awareness [77]. Overall they concluded that surfaces that could be interacted with directly could positively impact team awareness.

Figure 4.7: Designing to support situation awareness when collaborators are at a distance. This system supports situation awareness by displaying arm shadows of remote collaborators. Source: [203]

Tuddenham and Robinson explored whether or not it was possible to maintain team awareness across remote tabletop conditions. Leveraging research on the value of pointing for maintaining situation awareness, they achieved situation awareness across remote locations by displaying the shadows of the arms of remote participants on tabletops as shown in Figure 4.7 [203]. Recognizing that reaching for objects would not always be feasible for users of larger tabletop displays, Pinelle et al. investigated a variety of virtual embodiments by which 'arms' might be displayed (other than arm shadows). In a task involving sorting pictures they found that all types of virtual embodiments helped to maintain situation awareness equally, but virtual embodiments were not treated the same way as physical embodiments by teams, and that people preferred more realistic *virtual* embodiments [154].

In studies of *remote* situation awareness where the entire team is distributed, and the use of visualizations in an analysis task, Balakrishnan, Fussell and Kiesler found that visualizations do improve synchronous remote collaboration, but particularly so if they are 'full access' and provide information to underlying data. They found this condition encouraged tool use and discussion [8, 9]. In a subsequent study that appeared to involve analyzing significantly more data, Balakrishnan, Kiesler, Kittur and Fussell showed that sharing a visualization of all the data, but constraining the amount of evidence available to remote collaborating pairs of analysts increased the amount of communication and reduced confirmation bias, producing better analysis outcomes [7].

Situation awareness is important for seamless, focused teamwork and shared displays have been used for enhancing situation awareness. Collaborative work co-located around a shared surface (either tabletop or wall-mounted) provides additional natural means of providing enhanced situation awareness because the surface itself brings teams in close proximity and direct team interactions with the surface are easily perceived. However, when collaborative teams are distributed, additional techniques are required. Visualizations can improve synchronous remote collaboration, but the details of how much to share are important to successful analysis outcomes. These details are determined by carefully studying an activity.

4.4.2 REDUCED ERROR RATES OR INCREASED COMMON GROUND

Mixed-display environments are more complex, but can also solve many issues at the interaction level associated with document flow, input and pointing. In this next section, we review the research on the ability of mixed-display environments to support collaboration.

Sometimes, when considering team performance, an important issue can be the synchronicity or amount of common ground achieved within a team. This, for example, would be an important consideration if mission-critical decisions are being made by a team.

Wallace et al. studied teams completing a challenging collaborative optimization task using either a single large vertical display and one mouse per person or a mixed-display environment. His participants used laptops with mice and a large vertical screen. The display content was synchronized across the laptops and the large screen, meaning all displays were identical and showed each team member's cursor [219]. Six teams with three students per team used both setups and completed the optimization task under three different conditions. Each condition imposed different controls on user interactions when conducting the optimization tasks.

The researchers observed that the large display was rarely used when teams worked in the mixed-display environment as shown in Figure 4.8 on the left. In other words, the team dynamics changed completely with the introduction of synchronized laptop displays in comparison to the condition with mice as shown in Figure 4.8 on the right. There was a significant difference in error rates; the mixed-display environment teams committed fewer errors, and so this setup was seen as the more cognitively successful arrangement. However, the single large vertical display setup with multiple mice was better in terms of its ability to enable greater awareness of the actions of others, and therefore it was better at building common ground within teams. This implies there are trade-offs. To mitigate these, Wallace et al. explored imposing controls on interactions with objects to explore their impact on collaboration. They found that imposing controls on interactions with optimization tasks forced even greater situation awareness because it forced team members to interact more.

These results show that choosing to distribute an application across a single display or multiple displays can make a large difference in group performance, as can the software controls that define access to elements in the user interface. It also shows that there are trade-offs to be considered when pondering different arrangement of displays. In this case the trade-off was between supporting individual cognition and achieving reduced error rates, versus supporting team interactions and achieving greater common ground.

Figure 4.8: Teamwork in mixed-display environments. Wallace's first experiment comparing group work with one large display (right) and a mixed-display environment (left). The photo was taken from beside the large display, which is not shown. In the mixed-display environment the large display was hardly used. Source: [219]

4.4.3   SUPPORT FOR EXPLORING DATA

Sometimes exploration can be an important team objective. This could be the case in fact-finding missions where a significant amount of information requires exploration, or if exploring is required to find information.

In a follow-up study to their initial study, Wallace et al. asked 12 teams to complete the same collaborative optimization task using laptops and a shared display. The research goal was to discover the role of shared displays in collaborative settings [218]. In one condition, the large display was used to present the overall status of the task. In the other condition, the three laptops and large display again operated synchronously with one another. In either condition, team members could point on the large display by manipulating their laptop's cursors with mice. Two conditions for accessing scheduling tasks were tried. In one all participants had shared access, and in another they had to negotiate access for certain task types. One difference from previous studies was that team members could undo a last move and this proved to be an interesting innovation. In this follow-on study, there were no differences between the two display conditions on task performance, completion time, error rate, or efficiency. The addition of the undo command, however, encouraged exploration. Compared to the last study, the groups took a bit longer, produced much more optimal schedules, and talked a lot more. Their follow-on study showed that the addition of an undo command could encourage teams to explore more solutions and therefore find better solutions.

4.4.4   FLUID MOVEMENT AND AVAILABILITY OF WORK ARTIFACTS

In many work places artifacts are essential to the work and are primarily digital. During collaborative work, it is important that these artifacts be readily shared so they can be discussed, compared, reflected upon and so on. Much of the research conducted in mixed-display environments aims to enable this important feature.

Bachl et al.'s study involved a mixed display environment and four conditions for accomplishing a simple sorting task that required moving documents. In three conditions, the task required moving documents back and forth between a tablet and a large multi-touch tabletop display. The four conditions are shown in Figure 4.9. Participants preferred moving documents by pressing a button [6]. When comparing a mixed display environment and just a tabletop, they found that the mixed-display environment encouraged more diverse sorting strategies, but just the tabletop resulted in closer collaboration and better overall performance.

Figure 4.9: A sorting task in a mixed-display environment done three ways. Top left: just on a multi-touch tabletop. Top right: transferring documents from tabletop to tablet using a button (the preferred method). Bottom left: transferring documents by depositing them into a container. Bottom right: transferring document uses lenses. Source: [6]

Researchers at the University of Illinois and Microsoft aimed to create a multiple display environment (MDE) using a mixture of laptops and shared displays [21]. They wanted to be able to "place myriad information artifacts on shared displays for comparing, discussing, and reflecting on ideas; to jointly create and modify information to enhance focused problem solving or enable opportunistic collaboration; and to allow quick and seamless transitions between [individual and collaborative] modes of working." To achieve this their system had to have the ability to "create, share and exchange task information, to allow individual work in parallel and joint interaction, to allow seamless transitions between these work modes, and to maintain awareness of each other's activities." These goals had been achieved individually by previous systems, but never collectively, and they had never been tested in a real workplace environment. Their tool IMPROMPTU (seen in Figure 4.10) was created and trialled by two different Agile software teams, each of whom collaborated regularly and, during the course of those collaborations, shared many artifacts. One team was co-located in a team room and the other had co-located offices. In both cases, teams used the multiple display environments heavily in their collaborations. They shared documents in their original contexts to solve compiler errors, jointly reviewed code, co-wrote brief reports, integrated code into a repository, collaboratively took notes, posted interesting articles and so on. The researchers reported that tasks and documents moved readily between large displays and laptops, and individuals moved easily between parallel work and joint work.

Figure 4.10: IMPROMPTU moves documents between laptops and a shared display. The user interface for laptops: a) A column of collaborators. b) An area where a document is placed when a user wants to transfer it to a large display. c) Sharable attributes can be set. d) A replicated editable window. e) A replicated view-only window. Source: [21]

4.4.5   WORK IS MORE SATISFYING

The majority of studies that we read reported that participants enjoyed working with large displays. For example, a study of the NiCE Discussion Room (Figure 4.11) where 13 small co-located groups performed a 30 minute mixed-focus collaborative design task in an environment with a variety of digital surfaces returned positive results. It showed that participants were engaged, they transitioned smoothly between individual and collaborative work, they enjoyed the work, and they used many of the diverse resources of the room [78]. Participants used sketching walls, paper interfaces (Anoto technology) and laptop displays to move sketches and information seamlessly between these surfaces. As another example, Bachl et al. reported that participants in their study enjoyed using tablets in combination with tabletop displays to sort [6]. In fact participants enjoyed experiences even when applications were not specially designed, but merely adapted for large displays with multiple input mechanisms. Isenberg, Carpendale et al. retrofitted an application called NodeTrix with a traditional graphical user interface, which was originally designed for a single regular-sized display, to work with a large display output and multiple mice input. Their detailed description of the changes required to the software are instructive in themselves, but their study of groups of four experts performing social-network analysis tasks provided insight into the ease with which a large visualization could be used and the enjoyment that analysts could experience, even if the application was initially designed assuming a traditional interface paradigm with a single mouse and one regular-sized monitor. [92]

Figure 4.11: A specially designed collaboration room with a mixture of digital surfaces. The NiCE discussion room was created to enable design work. Source: [78]

4.5   THE IMPORTANCE OF GOOD DESIGN

All of the literature we reviewed in this chapter pointed to the importance of good design, but didn't clarify the consequences of bad design. Poorly designed surface applications for shared displays can degrade overall performance. Studies of multiple displays provide some insight. In studies conducted in a military context on collaborative mission-oriented tasks, mere duplication of a team member's private displays on a shared display in a misguided attempt to increase situation awareness *increased* mental workload and degraded team performance in high workload conditions [24]. Work on exploring varying arrangements of displays for teams engaged in an intellective sensemaking task showed that well thought out arrangements of displays in meeting spaces positively impacted a team's performance, the ability of the team to collaborate, and team satisfaction. This study also showed that the cognitive and social nature of the collective work could shift with different types of display arrangements, particularly if the environment contained mixed types of surfaces [156].

Some other studies have looked at surface technologies more specifically. In a study of a group sorting task accomplished in two conditions, one with a multi-touch tabletop and one with a multi-touch tabletop and tablets, researchers found a decrease in overall task performance and close collaboration when tablets were used in conjunction with the tabletop display, in comparison to just a tabletop [6]. This suggests that there should be a good reason for the introduction of tablets into a collaborative tabletop environment, not to mention good design work behind their introduction.

In another study about surfaces, Rogers and Lindley wondered whether a large horizontal interactive display, a large vertical interactive display or a single laptop was best for moderately complex group work involving planning, decision making, and accessing multiple sources of digital data. In a lab study of collaborating groups of students they examined how the physical arrangement of displays might impact social factors. They found there was an impact in terms of the roles individuals assumed at the display, idea generation, amount of discussion, coordination, control, group attention, and group awareness. Their results favored large displays for an improved social environment for collaboration versus a single laptop. Smaller differences were noted between large horizontal and large vertical displays, but in balance the horizontal displays were preferred for the type of task they studied, especially when they considered that additional devices like calculators and notepads (analog surfaces) were leveraged in the work. In this mixed digital and analog surface environment, the tabletop had some advantages over the vertical display because it was also used to hold calculators and notepads [166]. A careful consideration of this topic and *how* a shared tabletop and personal displays can be an aid to group processes can be found in Wallace's recently completed dissertation. He shows how certain arrangements and not others can be an aid to sensemaking tasks because they can help to prioritize materials, compare data, and form group hypotheses [217].

Surfaces in and of themselves do not necessarily provide advantages for collaboration, and careful design decisions are required to achieve the types of positive results that researchers are finding. When surface systems are properly designed, the findings are quite positive for the case that surfaces can enable collaborative analysis work.

4.6   NON-TRADITIONAL DISPLAYS FOR COLLABORATION IN ORGANIZATIONS

In the next few sections we turn away from lab studies to focus on industry and government experiences with large displays and mixed-display environments as reported in the literature. We report on several case studies of organizations and their experiences with developing or deploying innovative display systems to advance their work. We present experiences at organizations where a primary aspect of the work is analysis work, where the pattern of the work is mixed-focus collaboration pattern, or where the work relies heavily on artifacts.

iRoom: Effective use of large displays   At Stanford University Liston et al. observed professional design and engineering teams working in paper and 'mixed paper and digital' workspaces designing buildings [123]. They observed that paper-only meetings were qualitatively different in that they appeared to require more clarifications, digressions and grounding; the paper-only environments also left teams less satisfied with meeting outcomes.

In an effort to understand why the mixed environment was more successful, the Stanford researchers developed a very rigorous observation and analysis method and used it to compare two professional multi-disciplinary design teams at work on a building design project in a specially designed collaboration space called the iRoom. The iRoom was equipped with paper, a workstation with a regular display that was connected to the Internet, a whiteboard and two SmartBoards. The workstation was loaded with a building modeling tool. One team they observed using the iRoom had six months of experience with this building modeling tool in comparison to another team they observed that had only two months of experience.

Familiarity with the modeling tool and cleverness in overcoming some idiosyncrasies with Smartboards they were using appeared to make a difference in the way the teams used the room. The experienced team interacted with the Smartboard content with greater ease. They also developed an efficient process that leveraged large display technologies well, using them to systematically identify, annotate and store issues (essentially annotated screen captures). They then reviewed the annotated screen captures at the beginning of each meeting, to see if follow-up changes were adequate to address the issue raised in the previous meeting. Figure 4.12 shows the team in the process of following up on an issue raised at their previous meeting to assess whether or not the issue had been satisfactorily resolved by design changes since their last meeting. Their expertise and comfort levels with the SmartBoard and the modeling tool allowed them to smoothly explore the building they were designing. Their process was more effective than the less experienced team's process, where building features were explored systematically in the same order each time.

Both teams expressed satisfaction with the iRoom setup and liked the mixed environment. After an exhaustive analysis of every meeting action, the researchers were able to say that the more experienced team showed better focus, considered more alternative solutions, required fewer clarifications, resolved issues more rapidly, worked more rapidly, resolved more issues, left fewer unresolved issues, generated more suggestions, exhibited more positive emotions, made greater use of digital artifacts, and expressed greater satisfaction with their meeting outcome [123]. The less experienced team spent more time orienting themselves to problems before resolving them. Of course it's hard to tease out the influence of the team's experience level and the contribution of the iRoom setup, but the more experienced team claimed that the iRoom had saved them approximately three to five months of work.

This research demonstrates that mixed paper and digital workspaces can be very effective for productivity, and satisfying to use in challenging, artifact-rich environments where many con-

Figure 4.12: The iRoom is a collaboration room with a mixture of digital and analog surfaces. It is a design space for multi-disciplinary teams working on the design of a building. The left screen shows a snapshot of an issue identified in a previous meeting and the red rectangle shows annotations regarding the unresolved issue. The right screen shows solutions to the issue that the team is currently reviewing. Source: [123]

flicting aims must be resolved. However this research also demonstrates it can take teams some time to make effective use of mixed paper and digital collaborative workspaces.

MERBoard: Collaboration with maps and plans   NASA researchers implemented a large interactive work system called the MERBoard Collaborative Workspace that was used in the Mars Exploration Rover Missions. The system included personal computers and several distributed, large, touch-enabled plasma display systems with customized software that was connected to a centralized server and database. The goal of the system designers was to increase the productivity of five dispersed science teams (they spanned three floors) and to improve team and inter-team communications and collaborations in a high-pressure, time-critical, mission-based environment [200]. The system was to be used to support the hypothesis-driven analysis of rover data, tele-robotic science, and controlling the rover on Mars (See Figure 4.13 and 4.14). The researchers carefully determined system requirements by watching the various science teams at work during field tests of the real rover. The team designed a special-purpose system with a simple interaction paradigm that would support the scientists to interact naturally, share information more fluidly, and communicate more effectively using large displays.

Two field tests of MERBoard were conducted. On the first test the designers observed that the scientists made effective use of the map annotation capabilities of the MERBoard. A second test was conducted with two MERBoards, one placed in an analysis room, and the other in a larger room that supported inter-team planning events. In the analysis room they saw that the MERBoard very effectively supported one team's analysis of map data and that the scientists liked

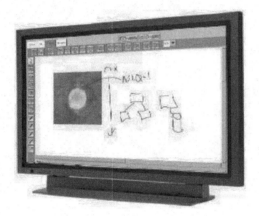

Figure 4.13: MERBoard: A large display touch-sensitive application designed for teams of Mars rover scientists. Source: [87]

Figure 4.14: MERBoards seen in a room in which many Mars Exploration Rover scientists worked. Source: [87]

interacting with maps directly through touch. In the planning room, they observed the scientists using the MERBoard to display a shared cross-team artifact called a process decision tree that controlled rover actions over the course of a day. They concluded that scientists gladly moved to digital representations from their previous paper-based representations because the MERBoard display space offered significant advantages. It was large, interactive, supported collaboration, and it allowed the scientists to save, recall, annotate and revise images and drawings.

This research shows that digital environments will be willingly adopted and work practices altered if the benefits of the digital aspects of the environment are superior to the previous environment. It also highlights the careful analysis and design work required to achieve this outcome even when providing basic functionality like annotating, saving and restoring data. However, another important lesson can also be learned from this system. When the rover mission actually happened, the MERBoards were barely used due to policy decisions regarding information-sharing at NASA that prohibited the transfer of certain essential files to the MERBoard server [87]. A lesson that can be derived from the unfortunate non-adoption of a useful system is that if it seems advisable, the design of systems should include wide consultation within an organization (including policy analysts) so that policies can be changed if necessary. Alternately, if the policy of an organization strictly prevents certain kinds of information sharing, then a collaborative environment must deliver benefits based only on those kinds of information that *can* be shared, a lesson that was articulated in 1988 by Grudin [71].

Sketchboard and Presentation Room: Artifact-centric work   In a recent paper, Buxton and colleagues report on over a decade of innovation with surfaces and interaction techniques for design studios [106]. Design environments are artifact-rich and highly collaborative. Buxton et al.'s paper tells a rich story of the transformation of a design studio environment from paper and tangible-only artifacts to mixed tangible and digital artifacts, and the careful and considered work of the designers who enabled this transformation. In this work designers created a number of applications for varying sizes of displays to support mixed-collaborative work. A principle they followed was that the "Choice of display size closely follows the physical needs of the activity." In their work domain, large displays were extremely valuable and they considered three sizes: large monitors, wall-sized displays and room-sized displays. Regardless of the application or task being supported, the designers focused on ensuring that they did not disturb the flow of face-to-face collaborative work with complicated interaction methods or interface devices. Instead, they aimed to enhance the flow of meetings and the flow of artifacts between activities. Always, they paid attention to the physical aspects of collaboration, such as natural movement, the comfort of collaborators, and the minutiae of considerations that result in effortless interaction with digital artifacts. This approach resulted in a number of innovations for car designers, but also some with broader applicability.

For example, Figure 4.15 shows an application called Sketchboard that was designed for mixed-display environments (tablets, laptops, large displays, and computer workstations) that allows collaborators to display relevant artifacts on a variety of displays depending on their needs. Artifacts are transformed on tablets in meetings, moved to large displays to be reassessed by a group, and then moved back to laptops or computer workstations when focused individualized work is required. The application helps the team to save and restore work, to replay the work they did, to annotate work and to leave messages for other absent designers. In short it makes design work flow more smoothly. Furthermore, once Sketchboard was shown to be valuable for supporting collaborative meetings, it was extended for use with a room-size display that was 64 feet long. In this incarnation they had to design new interactive mechanisms that allowed multiple people to interact with the visualizations on the room-sized displays directly. In this work they aimed to minimize visualize disruptions to viewers and physical travel for those interacting with images. This resulted in the creation of a mechanism to perform simple manipulations on an artifact at the far end of the display (such as resizing or moving) without having to physically move to it, and also a mechanism for remote pointing called Spotlight, which helped users draw attention to an image on a very large display by making it more brightly lit than all the other images.

Figure 4.15: Sketchboard: An application designed for a large display for groups that collaborate with many artifacts. The large display shown on left displays four drawing artifacts in a central area and smaller icons of other artifacts in a strip at the top. To the right is a closeup of a TabletPC display view. Designers in the meeting interact with the large display using their TabletPC and a stylus. They can flick artifacts back and forth between the large display and their TabletPC. Both displays show specially designed circular interaction menus. Source: [106]

Another application with broad applicability was a room-sized application that supported nervous or novice presenters called Presentation Room. This application cleverly used multiple displays (some for the audience, and some for the presenter) to help everyone know how far along the presenter was in the presentation, and to help the presenter stay focused on the audience and not the display contents [106].

Buxton et al.'s research is extremely valuable in its orientation to supporting collaborative work in the design industry. Exemplary practices demonstrated by the designers include their emphasis on the importance of maintaining workflow, eliminating technological hindrances, and to the evolutionary approach taken when creating tools to support collaboration. The results have been a significant change in the way work is conducted at design studios at many places around the world. In the opinion of the authors "the benefits of digitization are so great that traditional non-digital studios are no longer viable," but also that "many challenges still exist". Generally, the designers found that, at least in the domain of car design, when it comes to displays "bigger is better" probably because visualizations of cars can now be to scale. Further, their need for a large amount of contextual material that is easily accessible is accommodated by large display spaces because these can display many digital artifacts.

Many aspects of Buxton et al.'s work could be leveraged in the analysis domain. One is the explicit support for collaboration through applications for large displays that easily allow the manipulation of digital artifacts. Another is the design of systems that have a low learning threshold and are intuitive to users, an approach that enables technophobic or novice users to participate. A final aspect of this work that should be leveraged is the emphasis on workflow, which is a strong commitment to ensuring that collaborative work using surface applications is focused on the work of a meeting and not on the technology that supports it.

Aspects: Mission critical work with mixed media   As a final example of a collaborative endeavor with a government agency, some research at the University of Waterloo focused on the development of tabletop systems to support Canadian Navy operations. This work began in 2006 when researchers conducted a 'hybrid' cognitive task analysis based on a realistic scenario encountered by mission commanders. This process generated an in-depth understanding of the activity-based situation awareness needs for this task [176]. From there the group developed two visualizations for a 42-inch wall-mounted interactive plasma screen. These displays allowed the mission commander (and their team) to visualize their area of interest and to develop a strike schedule for threats in that area [175]. Then a pen-based tabletop system was developed that incorporated different types of information such as maps, charts, and reports and a custom-designed interaction paradigm that afforded easy co-located work around a tabletop [174, 177]. Their system, called ASPECTS, was usability tested with 41 people who enacted the role of mission commander and gave positive reviews. Subject matter experts also evaluated the system favorably. Figure 4.16 shows the setup of the system in a room and Figure 4.17 shows students using the application [178]. This ongoing project presents a good example of research-driven design work and also creates a realistic expectation of the steady progress that can be made when academia and government organizations collaborate, even when the areas of research are sensitive.

4.7   ISSUES ARISING

Research has clearly shown there are many advantages to using large displays for individuals. These include cognitive benefits, increased productivity, reduced errors, and greater satisfaction. We believe these benefits to individuals often carry over into collaborative situations. Research on groups and teams, however, is much newer. Early results are by and large very positive, but also indicate that it is very important that surface applications be carefully designed. For example, to increase situation awareness in contexts where groups are collaborating loosely, the research shows that it is very important to reduce the amount of information that is shared to no more than what

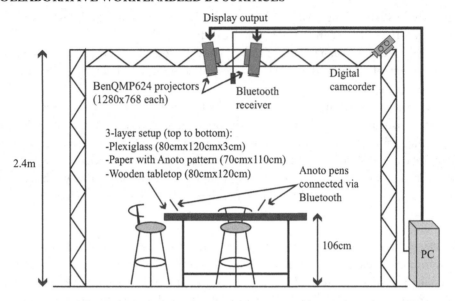

Figure 4.16: An interactive tabletop system using digital pen technology. Source: based on [174, 177]

Figure 8. A group using physical deixis (pointing) to group discuss a shared information window in the ASPECTS interface.

Figure 9. A group using the expansive workspace to create storage territories at the edge of the tabletop workspace.

Figure 10. A participant has arranged several ship information windows side-by-side to enable a visual comparison of the ships' available assets.

Figure 4.17: Students using the ASPECTS digital pen tabletop application. Source: based on [174, 177]

is required. Other research indicates the positioning and arrangement of displays can impact collaboration. In mixed-display environments the research shows that it would be important to be clear about the most important objectives of the collaboration so that choices about display devices and functionality can be made with these considerations in mind. Overall, the results for using surfaces to enable analytics are positive, but research in the area is still emerging and many avenues are unexplored.

CHAPTER 5

The Theory and the Design of Surface Applications

The goal of this chapter is to look at designing surface technology applications to enable collaborative analysis work through a variety of theoretical lenses to illustrate how those theories can be used.

5.1 THEORIES AND FRAMEWORKS

Theories operate at many different levels, such as organizational, socio-technical, social, or individual, and they provide a general orientation to research or design work. We use the term 'theory' loosely, using it to refer to frameworks, models and even a mantra! Theory can capture understandings from lab studies, field studies or simply years of experience in a field and it makes sense to leverage them. The correct theory to apply in any research project depends on the research questions and the background of the researchers. The fields from which theory can be leveraged in this domain are numerous.

We emphasize theories that reflect the types of research questions we have asked, which tend to be about collaboration, but other theories relating to the value of touch itself or the benefits of novel interaction techniques, would be useful for different research questions. For example, our research has not focused on generating new visualizations and therefore we do not review theories about visual perception. An example theory of visual perception is gestalt psychology, which takes a holistic view of brain functions such as perception. We imagine the various principles of this psychology may be of varying importance for large versus regular-sized displays. Similarly, our research is not about the judgments analysts make when working with visualizations. Therefore, we have not reviewed psycho-physical theories that would apply in these circumstances. Nor has our research focused directly on analytical thinking; we review some models, but some research on avoiding common pitfalls in human thinking (like jumping to conclusions) [101] would be very relevant. Clearly an exhaustive survey of relevant theories would be impossible.

What we try to do in this chapter is to show *how* theories can be applied. Whenever possible we try to provide examples where theories are applied to the problem of developing software systems for analysis or collaborative analysis, and where the interface is a large display or a surface, and which may involve the use of visualization techniques.

We first touch on theories about individual and collaborative analysis work that rely on visualizations because it seems that visualizations are essential to analyzing 'big data,' a major challenge of our times. Then, because there is little theory about collaborative analysis work and understanding collaboration is important, we review general theories about collaboration and show how they can be applied to the problem of designing surface applications.

In this next section we look more closely at theories that reflect understandings of individual and collaborative analysis work, many of them providing understandings of the value of interactive visualizations.

5.2   MODELS OF INDIVIDUAL ANALYSIS

Reasons for working with visualizations: Amar and Stasko looked at the reason for working with visualizations, suggesting that they helped to bridge two gaps (Figure 5.2) [3]. The Worldview Gap lies between an analyst's perceptual processes and their cognitive process, which results in their perception of useful relationships. To bridge this gap, the analyst must be able to collect useful data, create useful views, and *understand* those views, which involves generating useful hypotheses. The Rationale Gap lies between the point where the analyst has perceived useful relationships and then must *explain* them. To bridge this gap, the analyst must describe their confidence in the data and in the perceived relationships. To bridge either gap, the analyst can use visualizations. We next review various models that show how interacting with visualizations helps analysts perceive useful relationships in data.

Human behavior when using visualizations: Information visualization for analysis has a long history, but the early history is dominated by static diagrams and graphs. Dynamic visualization is more recent, powered by computers and software for data processing and graphical display. Dynamic visualization design involves the design of the user interaction, where user behavior changes the visualization. This behavior was discussed and developed on a case-by-case basis in many early schemes for dynamic information visualization, for example by Shneiderman and his colleagues in the design of Treemaps [182], Starfield displays [2] and Lifelines [155]. These visualizations are useful but it is not our purpose to describe them here, rather we consider the behavioral processes involved. Shneiderman addressed this more general issue by identifying the patterns of behavior that emerged in using such visualizations, and offered a taxonomy linking behavior and types of visualization [181]. He proposed the following visual information-seeking mantra: "overview first, zoom and filter, then details on demand" as a general guideline for behaviors that enable visual thinking. But he also identified common operations that are required when working with visualizations. These include transforming data, providing an overview of a collection, zooming in, filtering items, accessing details of items on demand, relating items, undoing, replaying, and redoing, refining, and extracting items of interest. This taxonomy and its rationale have given rise to further evaluation and refinement of designs for dynamic visualizations. An example of a refined Treemap by Bederson, Shneiderman, and Wattenberg is shown in Figure 5.1. Treemaps show complex information in nested rectangles to show both hierarchy and aggregation in a constrained 2D space, and allow filtering, scoping, and inspection of de-

Figure 5.1: This visualization of hierarchical structures helps users acquire an overview of the data of interest, access detailed values, compare nodes and sub-trees to find patterns and exceptions. The Treemap depicts the contents of ACM Interactions magazine pictorially. Source: [15]

tails, as described in the mantra; the refinements address how to preserve order that helps the user stay oriented throughout such a dynamic process. Further examples of the interplay between visualization and behavior are available in Benderson and Shneiderman's book [14].

Human cognition when using visualizations: In contrast to behavioral understandings, other researchers have sought to understand what is happening cognitively when analysts interact with visualizations. William et al. suggested that when analysts interact with visualizations they engage in a *dialogical* inquiry (an internal dialogue with the external data) [224]. In their view, the modes of inquiry of the human mind act in mutual synchrony with interactive visualizations, each mutually influencing the other in a kind of unspoken dialog. Thinking happens as the dialog between the analyst and the visualization unfolds (i.e., as the visualization is explored). To apply this theory when designing tools for analysts, the designer matches their understanding of the analyst's goals and tasks with the representational and interactional intents of the visualization tool. The aim is that the visualizations and interactive methods be in 'sync' with the natural modes of inquiry of the human mind. Natural modes of analytic inquiry include deductive, inductive, and abduc-

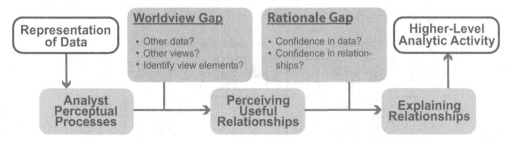

Figure 5.2: Two unrecognized gaps in the visualization process of the analyst. Shown are the world-view gap and the rationale gap. The three steps are (roughly speaking) seeing, understanding, and explaining. Source: based on [3]

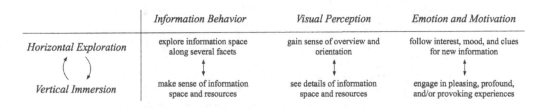

Figure 5.3: The information flaneur. This table shows the relationship between 'horizontal exploration' and 'vertical immersion,' two activities the 'information flaneur' engages in when exploring large data sets. Source: based on [56]

tive reasoning, and working with hypotheses. The analyst's goal is 'meaning making' and from a dialogical perspective analysts are seen as 'meaning makers.' From this understanding, without interactivity there cannot be a rich dialog and therefore analytic thinking is severely hampered.

Human behavior when analyzing large data sets: Thinking about how analysis work is changing in the light of the challenges presented by large data, Dörk et al. have suggested that a more appropriate model for today's analyst is an 'information flaneur,' a person who is curious, creative and critical in their approach to seeking information, pursuing multiple lines or facets, and driven by loose hypotheses [56]. This puts the emphasis on 'horizontal exploration,' i.e., finding the right set of information to analyze in balance with 'vertical immersion,' which is making sense of information and resources. Their model of the relationship between these two activities is shown in Fig 5.3. While traditionally tools have been designed for the 'vertical immersion' step, examples of interactive visualizations designed with the idea of exploration in mind are Thudt's et al.'s Bohemain bookshelf [196] and Dörk et al.'s multi-touch application EdgeMaps shown previously in Figure 2.21.

Human cognition when analyzing large data sets: Visual Analytics emerged around 2004 out of the needs of biologists and those engaged in national security. This multidisciplinary approach to analysis work aims to bring the field of cognition, design, scientific decision-making and other areas together to understand and develop systems for analysts working with large data sets. It views visualizations as essential aids to analysis work focusing on analytical reasoning abilities in interaction with visualizations and how these two elements in combination impact decision-making outcomes [195, 228].

Although there is a strong debate about the value of theory of visualizations in the field of Visual Analytics [52, 113], some theories have been applied. A tool called In-Spire was developed using a theory of 'satisficing' proposed by Simon Herbert in 1947. This theory explained the common phenomena of analysts focusing prematurely on a likely hypothesis. In-Spire helps analysts select relevant documents from very large document sets [80]. It explicitly aimed to support convergent and divergent thinking by helping analysts find relevant documents as well as documents that challenge their views. In this way it worked against confirmation biases, the human tendency to prematurely settle on an initial hypotheses and seek evidence to support it.

Show Data Columns	Sort Hypotheses	Sort Evidence					
▼		Credibility	Classic spy who passed classified info 6	Archived data for LANL as instructed 3	Stashing Intellectual Property for his next job 1	Talked to Chinese but passed no classified info 1
WHL's wife was FBI/CIA Informant		Credible	Inconsistent	N/A	N/A	Neutral
WHL had a record of cooperating with the FBI and CIA		Credible	Inconsistent	Consistent	N/A	Consistent
Massive amounts of material were transferred to UNCLAS disc drives		Credible	Very Consistent	Consistent	Very Consistent	Very Consistent
WHL admitted he had disclosed sensitive info to a foreign govt		Credible	Inconsistent	N/A	Consistent	Consistent
WHL did not report all his meetings		Credible	Very Consistent	N/A	N/A	Consistent
PRC's W-88 sketch had revisions made after WHL lost access		Credible	Inconsistent	N/A	N/A	Consistent
99% of W-88 info on the Internet		Credible	Neutral	Consistent	Inconsistent	Consistent
No proof any classified documents were passed to the PRC		Credible	Inconsistent	Neutral	Neutral	Consistent
WHL was in regular contact with senior Chinese nuclear scientists		Credible	Consistent	Consistent	Consistent	Consistent
Entered lab at 0330 Christmas Eve		Credible	Very Consistent	Inconsistent	Consistent	Inconsistent
Did not download user manuals		Credible	Inconsistent	Inconsistent	Consistent	Neutral
Took computer files home		Credible	Very Consistent	Inconsistent	Very Consistent	Very Consistent
Moved files to UNCLAS computer		Credible	Very Consistent	Very Consistent	Very Consistent	Very Consistent

Figure 5.4: A table supporting an Analysis of Competing Hypotheses. Hypotheses with high values have been more strongly disproved. Hypotheses with low values are most likely if they are also consistent with the evidence. Source: based on [81]

Heuer, also taking a cognitivist perspective, focused on averting weaknesses in human reasoning [81]. Chief among his concerns was that the analyst's mental model tends to act as a filter on the information collected, and also on the strategies taken to analyzing information. This then introduces bias into the analyst's work even before visualizations become useful aids. From this perspective what is required are analytical tools that expose the analyst's hypothesis, their assumptions and chains of inferences in their thinking. He has also suggested that tools should be designed to expose alternative points of view. To this end, he designed a table containing alternative competing hypotheses, evidence, and evaluations of evidence (ACH is shown in Figure 5.4). Putting these tools into context, he imagines ACH and other tools will support a range of activities including analytic debates, brainstorming, devil's advocate work, competitive analysis, and internal and external reviews. Cluxton and Eich's tools combine ACH with tools that provide visualizations of evidence [42].

This very broad review of theories relating to individual analysis work has exposed significant diversity. We next turn to understandings of collaborative analysis work.

5.3   MODELS OF COLLABORATIVE ANALYSIS

Isenberg et al. observed co-located students analyzing in pairs and triples and discovered that group analysis work included the following seamlessly integrated phases: organizing the work, working in parallel and working jointly [95]. They also identified eight common 'processes:' browsing, parsing, discussing in a collaborative style, establishing task strategy, clarifying the meaning of a visualization, selecting appropriate visualizations, operating on a visualization, and validating a solution [96].

Chin et al. studied individual and collaborative intelligence analysis in the lab, but with real analysts. Their study did not produce a model, but a rich description that could provide valuable insight for designers. It showed that individual analysts adopt varied strategies. It discussed the time pressures involved in the work and the challenges of collecting, highlighting, tagging, and triaging information. The tools of the trade were maps, sketches, graphs and timelines, and sometimes annotated calendars and spreadsheets. The researchers reported that the analysts were very positively inclined to collaborative work and the paper describes the additional benefits of collaboration [38].

Because understandings of collaborative analysis work are few, we next look at broader theories of collaboration and how these have been applied to analysis work.

5.4   UNDERSTANDINGS OF COLLABORATIVE WORK

In broad research areas such as this one the application of theory can be challenging. Grudin and Poltrock addressed this topic in the field of CSCW (Computer-Supported Cooperative Work), a field that sees surfaces as one of many potential collaborative aids. In the application of theory to research, they have observed that when theory is used, it is more to present an argument than to build on a theory or test it. They "identify four distinct roles of theory in CSCW: (a) there is some traditional theory development through hypothesis-testing; (b) a theory's use as a referent can support efficient communication among people familiar with its terminology and constructs; (c) a theory can motivate or justify system architectures or development approaches; and (d) theory can serve as a guideline or checklist for researchers or systems developers" [73]. We next review some general theories of collaboration.

5.4.1   DISTRIBUTED COGNITION

The theory of distributed cognition developed by Hutchins and Kirsh addresses cognition within socio-technical systems. It is focused on technologies and is relevant for analyzing collaborative analysis work enabled by surfaces. Central to this theory is an understanding of cognition occurring over time and located in the tool-mediated interactions between individuals in an environment that together comprise a single cognitive system. The elements of a socio-technical system are the individuals, tools, and the environment. The focus of the analysis is the functional relationship between elements over time. The cognitive process is understood to unfold in a series of events that may or may not be a consequence of human agency (events may be triggered by machines). The entire socio-technical system is seen to accomplish various cognitive functions, duplicating human cognition and actions, but at the level of the socio-technical system. In this view, for example, databases are like human memory and querying a database is like remembering.

The distributed cognition perspective looks at what is understood about cognitive processes in the human mind, such as remembering or decision-making, and articulates how these are distributed across people and things so that systems such as cockpits are seen as being able to "remember their speed" [90]. It also puts a strong emphasis on embodied cognition (which emphasizes the mind body connection) and recognizes the vital role that tools have in both constraining and abetting human thinking and human actions in the world. As such, distributed cognition is a very good theoretical perspective for studying small group interactions mediated by either tangible or digital artifacts.

Distributed cognition has been proposed as a foundational theory for designing collaborative socio-technical systems [82, 109, 110]. A good description of a method for design that leverages this theory is provided by Rogers [165]. Her analysis technique focuses on people, their communications, and their interactions with tools and media. Using this method, the analyst notes how information is communicated and transformed by individuals and devices. An explanation of the distributed problem-solving activity is produced and the role of various mechanisms for sharing knowledge is highlighted. Problems and breakdowns are identified. These point to places in the system (communication mechanisms, protocols, or artifacts) that could be redesigned to improve the system's cognitive functioning.

Nobarany et al. used distributed cognition to design a collaborative visual analytics system called AnalyticStream [146]. Analysts worked collaboratively through this tool rather than face-to-face. The tool allowed analysts to reuse reasoning artifacts such as hypotheses, evidence, and causal relations. It aimed to help analysts piece together disparate data such as immigration records, travel patterns, phone calls, names, affiliations and locations. By considering their collaborative system as a cognitive process that performed various sub-cognitive processes like remembering, attending, reasoning and listening, they were able to design a system that was particularly good at distributing both attention and memory mechanisms across the digital and human elements of the system, relieving humans of taxing aspects of their work. Awareness of each others' efforts helped collaborating analysts reuse each other's products. Mechanisms for

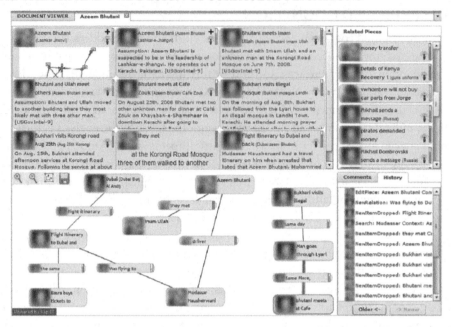

Figure 5.5: An intelligence analysis tool designed using distributed-cognition theory. A screen dump of the tool AnalyticStream that shows an analysis of fictitious person Azeem Bhutani in a Narrative view (top), Graph view (bottom), Related-Pieces panel (top-right), History panel (bottom-right). Source: [146]

'getting attention' also facilitated collaboration. A 'reminder' system, that six skilled analysts who tested the system particularly valued, drew attention to the relevant work of other analysts as it was completed. A snapshot of the interface is shown in Figure 5.5, which shows various helpful visualizations and the history mechanism. The view that the entire socio-technical system was active in the analysis work provided a unique perspective to tool development.

Also using distributed cognition, Plaue and Stasko [156] studied a data-intensive collaborative analysis task and analyzed it to understand how multiple display environments (MDEs) helped with analysts who worked face-to-face. To test their ideas about small group analysis work, 17 groups of six students came together in a meeting room that varied only in the way shared displays were arranged. The groups worked on a standardized analysis task. All meeting configurations had a whiteboard 'display,' but in one configuration there was also a single shared display, in another configuration there were two side-by-side displays, and a third configuration contained two opposing displays. Individuals could mirror their private display on a shared electronic display by a simple click of a button. The researchers studied performance, collaboration and satisfaction.

They found that the side-by-side displays improved performance even if the displays were a mixture of digital and analog displays (in this case a whiteboard). They also found that the nature of the intellective work was distributed differently across people and artifacts if the second display was analog. They concluded that both the physical nature and the arrangement of displays mattered. Comparing side-by-side digital and the digital-and-whiteboard display conditions they found that the flow of collaboration was less abrupt with the side-by-side digital condition, because it better enabled sharing, comparisons and exploration. They also found that side-by-side digital displays were most satisfying for analysis work.

Working from the perspective of distributed cognition helped these researchers keep their eye on the big picture—the overall functioning of the socio-technical system for analysis work—without losing track of the cognitive elements of this system (like attention and how the intellective work was spread across various surfaces).

5.4.2   EVOLUTIONARY PSYCHOLOGY

Researchers in the field of evolutionary psychology, such as Tomasello, have determined that people have evolved abilities and inclinations to collaborate; Tomasello calls this humanity's greatest strengths [199]. A good question that follows is whether or not surface applications can be designed to align with what is known about the human inclination to collaborate.

Yuill and Rogers used Tomasello's detailed and extensive scientific work on cooperative animal behavior and human collaborative behaviors to understand how large surfaces could naturally support the evolved and now innate cooperative and collaborative abilities of human teams.

In Tomasello's understanding the distinctive human ability to collaborate is achieved by leveraging the *shared intentionality* (the altruistic intentions based on the ability of humans to share) of groups or teams to achieve their shared aims [199]. This makes shared intentionality a very important aspect of situation awareness as it seems that without it, we cannot collaborate. But shared intentionality does not just happen, it is based on the evolved human ability to attend to social activity, to be aware of the actions and intentions of others, to take in background information, and to cooperate [234].

Leveraging these powerful understandings from evolutionary psychology Yuill and Rogers found that being able to attend to social activity, being aware of the actions and intentions of others, taking in background information, and cooperating are all feasible achievements for collaborators using tabletop systems. However, Yuill and Rogers provide an important insight that transform Tomasello's understandings into design principles for tabletop systems.

As a result of their experience as researchers and designers, they suggest that the three design issues that are most important for tabletop systems are the mechanisms for enabling the awareness of others' actions and intentions, control mechanisms in the interface, and the availability of background information. Developing guidelines, they claim tabletop systems will enable collaboration if applications for surfaces or systems of surfaces are designed to not just enable, but to *appropriately enable and constrain* social awareness, background information, and the control mechanisms of the interface that allow for cooperation. Their generalized framework of mechanisms and constraints for the design of tabletop applications emphasizes trade-offs regarding how much freedom and constraint should be designed into a system's physical, digital and social features, which the authors say is determined by contextual factors.

"For example, if the goal is to help users to learn to take turns, as might be the case for a tabletop application for kindergarten children, then the framework could be used to design in only weak constraints, presenting challenges so that the children develop an understanding of how and why to take turns. Similarly, if the goal is to enable older or more socially-skilled users to play a tabletop game, the constraints can be relaxed by building in opportunities for users to regulate their own turn-taking, for example, by allowing single touch by any user. This provides high constraint in control (only one user at a time) but no constraint on which user, so the group can only work together if there is some agreement about how control is shared. In a situation where users are in competition to contribute, it may be apt to impose a strong constraint to enforce turn-taking" [234].

Several examples in their paper that are based on tabletop applications they have developed show how design choices made by designers of surface applications can work for or against the natural collaborative abilities of people [234]. Their new design guidelines were tested against these previous designs to see if they could effectively generate design rationale. Moving forward, their understanding of this theory and their new guidelines will be used to augment their previous process where they would design instinctively, trial the design, reflect on errors they made, and then repeat the process. The theory-driven aspect will presumably help them arrive at better designs more quickly.

In the context of the analysis domain and in particular for intelligence analysts, designers may wish to introduce control mechanisms on artifacts, so for example artifact owners retain the sole rights to editing. Alternately, designers may wish to design available background information carefully to align with security policies; e.g., they may decide no documents with restricted access would be displayed if collaborating personnel did not have clearance. It may also be very important to know who was acting or had acted on artifacts, i.e., that there be an audit trail, and therefore interaction mechanisms that could tie an interaction to a person could be very valuable. According to Yuill and Rogers' deployment of evolutionary psychology, this sort of careful design of constraints would enable rather than impede collaboration in the intelligence domain.

5.4.3   ATTENTION MECHANISMS AND CO-LOCATED WORK

The human attention system is highly complex [58]. Despite over 100 years of research, our understanding of the exact limits and capabilities of the attention system are not yet fully known, as it encompasses a complex neural network spanning large areas of the brain. Before mentioning the role it plays in group work and in social environments, we review some of the known attributes and theories governing attention, particularly where it concerns the visual system, since it plays a major role in social interactions and shared environments.

From a cognitivist perspective, attention can be described as a mechanism which enables higher level processing to occur, such as recognition and memory [227]. Awareness is, in effect, the transference of high-level cognitive resources in order to better process a stimulus. If someone is attending to some stimuli, they are enabling high-level resources to work on that stimuli and are thus enabling awareness of it. In the human visual system there are several phases to processing visual stimuli, chief among them are the pre-attentive phase and the attentive phase.

The pre-attentive phase is a critical component of the overall attention system since it is extremely fast and typically deals with large sets of stimuli. Things which 'pop-out' are said to have been successfully processed in our pre-attentive phase, an example of which is demonstrated when looking for a circle among a set of triangles. In this case, we don't have to attend to the individual shapes within our field of view because the circle has very different characteristics from a triangle—it is both curved along the edges and does not match the three-edged pattern. Pre-attention enables attention to occur, but it does have well-documented limits, in particular a limited capacity and a bounded processing time.

The attentive phase also has a limited capacity and a bounded processing time. Obviously, the capacity of the attentive phase is much smaller than the total input of stimuli to the visual cortex or it would be theoretically possible to see everything and process everything in our field of view. It is sometimes possible to determine where someone is attending based on the direction of their eye gaze, as this is the principal way that higher level processing can occur. For example, object recognition takes place based on the fine details gathered by the fovea of the eye. It is not necessary, however, for the gaze to be very precise in order for attention to be given to an object. Consider, for example, the case where someone is walking and staring straight ahead, but is actually attending to some object perceived to be a threat off to the side, perhaps in preparation for it to make a sudden movement. In that case, the individual is splitting their attention between two things—just enough attention in the forward direction to allow for walking, and peripheral attention to quickly detect movement of a potential threat.

A psycho-physiological perspective proposes there are three different networks of attention:

1. *Alerting network*: used when constant sensitivity to the stimuli of the subject is required.

2. *Orienting network*: used to select or filter for stimuli.

3. *Executive network*: the wakeful part of attention for monitoring and resolving conflicts.

Each network is crucial to the normal operation of the attention system. Figure 5.6 shows where the three networks of attention (alerting, orienting and executive) exist in the brain [158]. In some cases the extent and location of these networks have been determined by the study of patients with brain injuries, and in other cases through the use of functional neuroimaging. A test called the Attention Network Task/Test (ANT) can be used to determine the capabilities of the networks. This test uses reaction time from responses to specific stimuli in order to measure the speed and efficiency of a particular attention system. This can be used to detect any abnormal development in children and the potential loss of function in those with brain injuries.

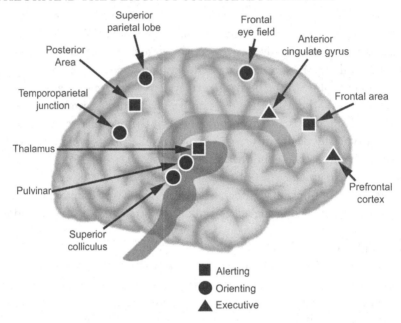

Figure 5.6: A biological perspective on attention. Areas of the brain where the three major networks of attention are situated. Source: based on [158]

The consequence of all this is that there are known biological limits and constraints to attention for each individual, with some people having better performing networks than others. Therefore when coming up with a system for sharing or collaborative work, the system must take into account these limitations and differences. For example, it is unlikely that two individuals can attend to all the information at once on a large display if processing the information provided requires more than just pre-attention. If the collaborative tasks are simply location-based problems where some item must be uniquely identified among a large body of easily distinguishable items, then the designer of such an application must only determine how to display items so that they are easily distinguishable. This strategy will minimize the time needed to locate items using pre-attention. However, in practice, most problems require high-level processing and therefore require more than just pre-attention, and fall into the realm of attention *and* awareness problems.

In the realm of shared spaces and large displays designers must focus on the potential problems of unintentionally masking or drawing attention to things which do or do not need to be attended to. The use of popups in normal computer use is an example of a designed element that can easily steal attention, as the sudden appearance of an object somewhere roughly in the field of view of the user is very likely to grab the user's attention. In terms of shared spaces, if one person is speaking too loudly it can often drown out and 'steal' the attention from nearby persons. Thus, careful consideration must be taken to not only the layout of spaces and the desired behavior of individuals in shared spaces, but also potential points of attention conflict or attention efficiency.

For example, a study conducted done by Berggen et al. showed that 'emotional' information influences attention more than neutral information, and that anxiety has a performance cost on attention [17]. These problems could be detected using eye-tracking and, in fact, eye-tracking itself is often used as a study tool in understanding the psycho-biological aspects of attention, possibly in combination with functional Magnetic Resonance Imaging (fMRI) and Electroencephalogram (EEG).

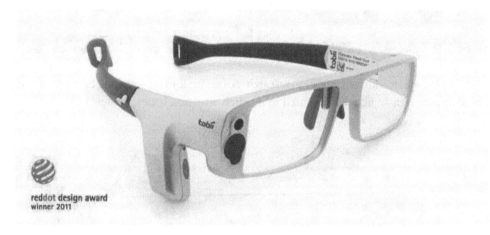

Figure 5.7: A head mounted eye-tracker made by Tobii.

Eye-tracking involves the use of technology to determine the location of a person's gaze. As a research tool, eye-tracking has gained considerable ground in recent years, mostly due to the reduced cost, increased capability, and increased availability of eye-tracking systems [173]. The Swedish company Tobii Technology has been a very active company in producing devices [198]. The combination of cheaper and more powerful camera sensor technology and Open Source frameworks, such as the ITU GazeTracker, allows researchers to build custom systems which behave to their own specifications and at a relatively low cost [70]. While early eye-trackers allowed tracking only within a specific visual range, such as single computer display, there are now alternatives. In particular, head-mounted eye-trackers, such as the Tobii device shown in Figure 5.7, allow more general tracking appropriate to collaborative work and diverse locations for attention.

Eye-tracking technology that is currently easily obtainable and easily configured can potentially add a lot of value to studies of social interaction. Even a basic mapping of eye movements to a video stream from a forward facing camera mounted on a person's head can give researchers knowledge of eye movements in relation to the person's perspective of the world, and the locus of their attention. Figure 5.8 shows an example. Video recordings showing the actual gaze points can also be used for conducting research on attention dynamics, and also for various pratical applications beyond research, such as in teaching, as for improving one's own ability to perform a task.

Figure 5.8: Using eye-tracking in attention research. An example of eye-tracking being used to display the locus of attention in an image being used to research attention issues. Source: [67]

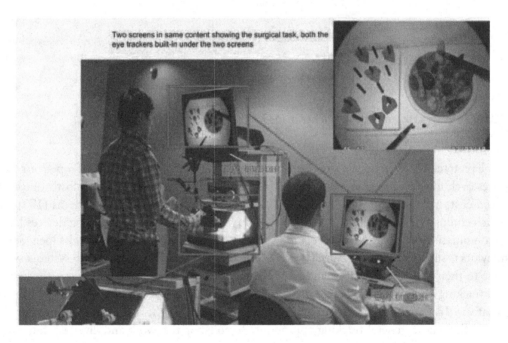

Figure 5.9: An eye-tracker used to help train surgeons in laparoscopic surgery. Source: [37]

The combination of ongoing research into how people typically attend to things in social interactions (or how attention changes in times of stress or emotion) and the use of eye-tracking to record eye movements has the potential to improve co-located work. Eye-tracking can also be a very useful tool in training and in easing shared tasks, as it allows individuals to attend to areas of interest in a more focused manner, or to split attention efficiently (Figure 5.9). It has been successfully used both in pair-programming and in parent-child reading tasks to help give an idea of where the expert is looking, or where the novice is looking [75, 152]. It is therefore not a stretch to suggest that eye-tracking has relatively untapped potential in training others for fairly complex work which requires a trained eye or multiple perspectives. Jobs which may take years of experience to develop proper skills, such as analysis work, could be helped by using this technology to leverage the expert-novice transfer of knowledge and experience. Eye-tracking data could help novices understand expert behavior directly, or it could be used to create models of expert behavior. This principle may also help analysts learn to analyze large sets of data more effectively.

Research into these areas is ongoing and looks to have promising results for future understanding of human attention and how it can be applied to complex collaborative environments.

5.4.4   GROUP SITUATION AWARENESS

Situation awareness is a field of study concerned with the perception of complex, dynamic and often highly technical environments. Mostly these environments are highly collaborative. For group situation awarness to occur the transfer of information is a primary goal. A situation awareness perspective considers how well a system supports knowledge transfer taking into consideration its importance and clarity. In other words, this perspective asks whether or not the system helps to clearly convey critical information needed at the precise time that it is needed. Systems designed to efficiently support the transfer of knowledge to and between users while they perform other tasks with high cognitive loads are said to support situation awareness. The roots of situation awareness are tied closely to the domain of aviation, but with advances in technology the need for situation awareness is now critical in many fields ranging from control rooms to collaborative data analysis. Figure 5.10 illustrates the importance of processing data in the environment in order to enable humans to comprehend massive amounts of information [59].

Endsley defines situation awareness as "the perception of the elements in the environment within a volume of time and space, the comprehension of their meaning and the projection of their status in the near future" [59]. Her understanding of situation awareness is that it is embedded in a dynamic decision making process [59]. She describes situation awareness as the combination of the following three levels of awareness:

1. *Perception:* The perception level addresses the ability of people in the system to absorb information from their surrounding environment, but also their awareness that they might be missing critical information.

2. *Comprehension:* The comprehension level addresses how well people can identify, store and retain information perceived in level 1 awareness and understand its meaning.

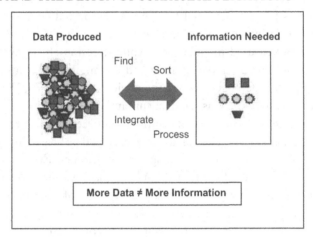

Figure 5.10: Situation awareness is achieved by filtering data. Only a minor subset of the team's data is required to support situation awareness. Source: based on [59]

3. *Projection:* The projection level addresses how people can leverage their understanding of level 2 information to intelligently predict or forecast future events and understand the potential impact of those events.

Kulyk et al. [116] extended Endsley's [62] three levels of situation awareness depicting situation awareness as an ongoing process that is part of collaboration. They emphasized the role of visualizations in maintaining situation awareness. The additional aspects of situation awareness they have identified follow:

4. *Previous knowledge and understanding:* This level addresses a person's previous knowledge and understanding which contributes to their ability to identify the source and nature of relevant events and information.

5. *Detection and comprehension:* This level addresses a person's ability to detect and comprehend relevant perceptual cues and information from the environment, especially the comprehension of multiple visualizations in their context.

6. *Interpretation and continuous reconfiguration:* This level addresses a person's ability to interpret visualizations and continually reconfigure their understanding and knowledge during collaboration. This addresses the ability of individuals to be aware of changes in the environment, as well as their ability to keep track of work in progress.

With respect to situation awareness, their interest is on its impact on team collaboration and *shared situation awareness*, which they define as "the degree to which every team member possesses the situation awareness required for his or her responsibilities" [63]. With respect to shared situation awareness, Kylyk et al. are concerned with answering the following questions that relate to its impact on collaboration:

- How can we understand the impact of situation awareness on collaboration?

- How can we support shared situation awareness in collaborative environments?

- How can we leverage shared large format monitors to support shared situation awareness?

- How can new interactive systems and visualizations be designed and evaluated based on their ability to support shared situation awareness and how might these systems actually stimulate new and existing forms of collaboration?

Kulyk et al. also identify some key benefits of displaying visualizations on multiple large shared displays:

- Visualizations on a shared display encourage group discussions.

- The visualization of data on a shared display allows group members to quickly determine the quality of the information.

- Multiple visualizations may be needed and when used concurrently there must be a clear visual relationship between these visualizations so as to avoid group members from getting lost, from being distracted, or from being inflicted with change blindness, which occurs when the participants do not realize that the focus of the discussion has changed.

- When multiple shared displays are being used with multiple co-related visualizations, changes in a particular visualization should also trigger changes in other related visualizations.

Applying the theory of situation awareness in the context of analysis work is not new. For example, Salerno et al. of the Air Force Research Laboratory in the United States applied Endsley's theory of situation awareness (top-down) and a bottom-up analysis approach to a monitoring problem [169]. Their work highlighted the various roles of the analysts and the value of applying theory to developing tools for conducting a simultaneous top-down/bottom-up, model-driven, strategic analysis to emerging problem situations. To illustrate the potential of their ideas they considered the scenario where analysts were tracking events leading to the the first Gulf War. One hundred and forty key events leading up to the Gulf War that were sequenced in time were used as input to the simulation. In one part of the process analysts developed an awareness of the situation by building a high-level model of indicators of a potential crisis situation developing. Events and reports from the field sometimes signaled the presence of an indicator. In their simulation, as the situation developed (based on events that were indicators), various aspects of the model (represented by a graph) were colored. The colors gave a sense of the urgency of the emerging situation. Analysts interacting with the colored graph could find out more information about indicators (including original data) by clicking on a node. A sample graph showing only some of the nodes is shown in Figure 5.11. A larger display would obviously be able to make more of this graph visible providing a better overview, and multi-touch features would allow parallel explorations and comparisons of the original data behind alerts.

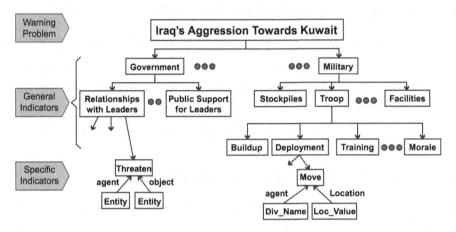

Figure 5.11: A framework for intelligence work using situation awareness theory. Sample graph that models indicators of a problem. This application helps analysts to be aware of emerging situations. Color is used to draw the attention of the analyst. Source: based on [169]

Situation awareness has also been used to develop tools to detect and investigate anomalous traffic between local networks and external domains. VisFlowConnect is a prototype application that discovers network traffic patterns in traffic flows between machines on a network leveraging the ability of the human mind to process visual information quickly [230, 235]. This tool was specifically designed to support situation awareness and is part of a larger toolkit called SIFT (another tool in this kit creates visualizations of the situation/activity on networks, subnetworks and machines). VisFlowConnect uses parallel axes representations and can help analysts become aware of denial of service attacks, virus outbreaks or port scans. The user interface is shown in Figure 5.12.

5.4.5   ACTIVITY THEORY

Activity theory is a broad framework that provides a cultural, social, developmental, and tool-centric perspective on people engaged in activities, including many aspects of previously mentioned theories. Activity theory was developed out of cultural-historical psychology and is often called CHAT (cultural-historical activity theory) [47, 51, 161, 220]. Cultural-historical psychology was founded by Lev Vygotsky (1896–1934), who studied human development through studies of human actions mediated by signs and tools [214, 215, 216]. Leontiev [121, 122], a prominant Russian psychologist and colleague of Vygotsky, developed the concept of *activity* to explain the

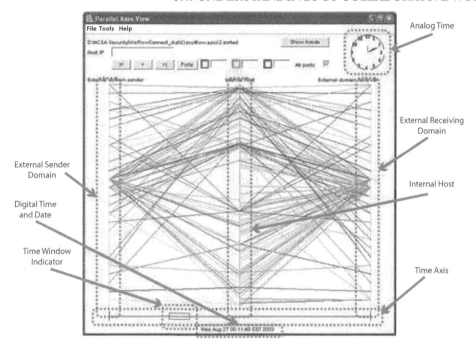

Figure 5.12: VisFlowConnect: A tool developed using situation awareness theory. This screenshot of VisFlowConnect shows analysts machines in external and internal domains ordered by IP addresses and 'flows' through the internal machines. Source: based on [230, 235]

broader context for mediated actions. He made activity the central unit of psychology claiming that the study of "activity, its construction, its development, and its transformations […] its various types and forms" was the way to understand human behavior because "human life is activity" [122] (p. 49). This is a strong statement, influenced by Leontiev's evolutionary psychological perspective, which led him to conclude that today humans meet their needs by developing and engaging in activities (either individual or joint). Activity theory now engages the interests of researchers from multiple disciplines and multiple countries [47, 51, 65, 221]. Since analysis projects are activities, and surfaces are potential tools that could enable them, activity theory can be used to provide understandings of analysis activities enabled by surface technologies. In the sections below we show how aspects of activity theory can inform the design of surface applications.

Activity theory can be applied in many ways in HCI research. As evidence of this diversity, in our own work we have used activity theory to understand the collaborative work of interaction designers and software developers from the perspective of individual collaborators [31]. As a result of a field study at eight organizations, we discovered that each collaborator creates a mental cognitive concept called an *interactional identity* that allows them to make their collaborative work meaningful and effective. It shapes the way collaborators use artifacts, see conflict in their work, understand their work relative to the project aims, and how they share joint tasks with their fellow collaborators. We also discovered that more experienced team members were more collaborative than less experienced collaborators. In effect, designers and developers mediated their desktop and tabletop interactions with each other through interactional identities which influenced their use of artifacts (e.g., documents, prototypes and so on). Given the way we observed our participants use of artifacts, we suggest that surface artifacts (digital documents and prototypes) should be flexible, and collaborators should be able to annotate and adapt them. This would allow collaborators to more easily employ their interactional identity in their interactions.

To use activity theory in design the first step is typically to identify and study an activity by conducting a field study. When gathering information the designer becomes aware of important 'objects' in the eyes of the people s/he is observing. These are likely to be the objects of activities. The object of an activity is the thing, person, or idea toward which the individual or individuals engaged in the activity direct their action; it is the central thing being transformed by those engaged in the activity. Having identified the object of the activity, the designer would then try to identify the motive for the existence of the activity (i.e., what human needs the activity meets), and through this process identify and name activities. Once an activity has been identified, a close examination of all aspects of the activity ensues, including roles that support it, tools, communication means, explicit and implicit rules, social norms, and cultural influences. Eventually an understanding emerges explaining why an activity is structured the way it is. This in-depth study of the entire activity provides constraints on its transformation. As an example of a field study, we used activity theory to create a model of the activities of operators in the complex work environment of operating centers, a domain of increasing importance in modern society [30]. We identified about ten activities including Incident Resolution and Monitoring Alerts. Many of these were regularly multi-tasked. We then used our model to speculate on the possibilities of using surface technologies to enable the work of the operators. By conducting field studies prior to developing surface applications, a broader picture of the cultural and social context and clear understandings of motives and constraints helps to ensure that the right surface applications are developed and the right surface technologies (tables vs. tablets and so on) are adopted.

Additional key concepts in activity theory are *actions* and *operations*. Individuals engaged in individual or group activities perform scripted sequences of goal-oriented actions that are achieved by sequences of operations, which are shaped by environmental structures and constraints. Surface computing involves many operations, structures and contsraints that are already commonplace in human activity. The structure and constraints of a 'surface' are ubiquitous and seen with blackboards, bulletin boards, meeting tables, and so on. Operations on those surfaces are also well-established and include placement, sorting, indicating, and gesturing with swipes and flicks. Moreover, many of these structures and operations are established in particular domain contexts. There is potential, therefore, for field studies to identify structures and operations already established in a domain that constitute opportunities for surface computing that will require little new learning, but offer advantages of automation and linkage to data and processing at scale.

A number of books have been written that detail an approach to HCI research and design using activity theory. We now highlight a few and say how these resources are of value to academics or designers interested in surfaces. We also provide examples where activity theory has been applied to understanding or designing surface technologies.

Bødker's book *Through the Interface* introduced activity theory as a guide for user interface design [23]. She argued for an interaction style which she called 'through the interface,' i.e., she claimed the ideal experience for users is that they perform goal-oriented actions (that advance their activities), but that they are not consciously aware of interface elements. Using activity theory she theorized that when users are forced to consciously attend to interface mechanisms to achieve their goals their work is negatively diverted and disrupted, and she provided a framework for analyzing these disturbances. We generally agree with this thinking, but also note that sometimes more sophisticated interface elements can be aids to conscious thinking. In the context of surface interfaces this approach would be similar to the ideal expressed in the term 'natural user interfaces' [223], but with added psychological underpinnings.

The book *Context and Consciousness* [143], an edited collection of articles and studies, presents activity theory as a theory of 'human practice' of value to the field of human-computer interaction [117]. The book emphasizes how environment (context) and thinking (consciousness) are intertwined through mediating artifacts, especially computer-mediated artifacts. It advocates field studies as a primary (though not sole) means to advancing the field of HCI. One study in this book is especially relevant to surface computing. Raeithel and Velichkovsky investigated how joint attention could be enabled [160] (a common goal for collaborative surface applications). Researchers observed paired experts and novices solve puzzles remotely. They found that providing mechanisms/mediators for facilitating joint attention on the task improved performance significantly. For example, in one study, being able to point improved performance by 40%. They also found that talk about solving the puzzle changed dramatically depending on the available mediators for enabling joint attention. To explain these differences, the authors hypothesized that experts were able to understand the perceptually different world of the novices, speculate about the novice's consciousness, and through this mechanism provide appropriate puzzle-solving advice to the novices. The relevance to surface computing is the emphasis on activities requiring joint work, joint attention, and the role of operations such as pointing. This kind of activity is directly supported by surface computing, where work around a large surface facilitiates joint attention, and pointing can be interpreted not only by the people involved, but also by the software.

The same orientation to enabling joint attention can also be used to design more sophisticated mechanisms for achieving joint attention with surface systems. This is what You, Luo and Wang did when they conducted their research on designing a presentation system using activity theory [233]. They designed interface elements that would enable the use of large interactive displays by experts who needed to present interactive material to novices. They developed paper prototypes which were tested by potential end-users who reenacted potential scenarios of use. Observing their concrete activity, they then reasoned about it by thinking about the activity's motive, object, roles, rules, etc. and by noting disturbances. Based on their reflections, they designed and then focus-group tested new interaction widgets. One widget was a type of context map that would allow presenters to easily rearrange content on their display while at the whiteboard, without obscuring the whiteboard for viewers. Another widget was a feedback mechanism for viewers whereby the presenter's gestures in the context map were duplicated in enlarged form on the large display, so viewers could see the presenter's gestures and therefore understand the reasons for changes in displayed images. These simple changes effectively resolved the disturbances they observed and enabled joint attention.

Activity theory was also described in a chapter in *HCI Models, Theories, and Frameworks* a compilation of articles edited by Carroll [18]. In this chapter Bertelsen and Bødker provide an extensive example showing how to apply activity-theory inspired methods to a design problem. Their example involved redesigning a graphical editor and simulator environment for colored petri-nets, which is a sophisticated and specialized analytic tool to describe distributed systems. They began by understanding that their tool would be used in two activities: the first in a professional context and the second in an educational context. In an educational context they felt the interface needed to be more visible, whereas in the professional context they felt it should be less visible. Their design moved away from an interface with overlapping menus and pull-down menus. Instead, their interface incorporated tool glasses, traditional tool pallettes, contextual marking menus, and two-handed input techniques. Details of the multiple, activity-based methods they applied to come to this conclusion are outlined in their chapter. Many of these would be readily applicable to a surface-based version of this application.

More recently, activity theory was highlighted in the 2nd edition of the *Encyclopedia of Human-Computer Interaction* [60]. Kaptelinin claims that "understanding and designing technology in the context of purposeful, meaningful *activities* is now a central concern of HCI research and practice". He says the emphasis in design is now on designing for a fuller and more meaningful human existence and activity theory is able to contribute. Kaptelinin presents activity theory as a second-wave, post-cognitivist HCI theory. To demonstrate activity theory's value in this regard, Kaptelinin describes its contribution to activity-centric (also known as activity-centred or activity-based) computing. Activity-centric computing postulates and creates extensions to traditional desktop systems. These help users who use their computing devices to engage in multiple activities to organize their digital resources in a way that more directly supports their diverse activities [210]. Researchers in the field have used the notion of 'projects' or virtual desktops to achieve this end. One study of the virtual desktop solution showed that this system provided a more satisfactory experience than traditional desktop environments [209]. Extensions of these concepts to surface technologies and collaborative work have yet to be envisioned, but may result in changes to the design of different surface devices to better support longer term activities, (i.e., ongoing projects) as well as shorter term tasks. Activity-centric computing and surface computing have similar structures, and may offer a kind of design-technology symbiois similar to that seen in the 1980s in the mutual success of early graphical user interfaces and object-oriented programming.

Very recently, Kaptelinin and Nardi published *Activity theory in HCI: Fundamentals and Reflections*. This book describes activity theory, the history of activity theory in HCI, and shows how it is valuable for advancing current issues in HCI. The authors also show how it has been increasingly adopted in HCI over the past decades. For example, they quote Carroll who claims that "the most canonical theory-base in HCI now is sociocultural, Activity Theory". As evidence of this claim they show there are 533 articles in the ACM Digital Library written from this perspective (more than for other perspectives). They claim that activity theory is relevant for 'emergent paradigms,' of which we'd argue surface computing is one. Their book provides many examples of well-designed systems, such as Matthews et al.'s framework for understanding, designing and evaluating peripheral displays [133] and Carroll et al.'s work on awareness and teamwork [36], both of which foreshadow how this approach can inform surface computing.

We began by saying that activity theory was a broad framework. We have touched on many ways that activity theory relates to surface computing. Of particular relevance are the focus on joint activity, typical in applications for large surface computing, and the recognition of the link between actions and operations, where similar links already exist in many domains suitable for surface computing. We also outlined studies and designs where activity theory has already been applied to the design of surface applications.

5.5   THE ROLE OF THEORY-ENABLED UNDERSTANDINGS FOR DESIGN

Theory can be useful for designing lab studies of collaboration. For example, tools, techniques, visualizations and devices can be studied for their impact on individual or collaborative analysis work. With controlled studies it's possible to study whether such elements have had an impact on avoiding errors, changing thinking patterns, or impacting attention. Lab studies can also be designed to study attention.

This chapter has also shown that theory can also be very fruitfully applied to novel design work. Many examples of this type of work were given in this section.

Whether the motive for a project is understanding or design, the point is that progress in understanding and evolving research work can be scientifically based if driven from a theoretical perspective. We believe this type of tool development is far more effective than design by intuition or unarticulated theories about how individuals or groups behave.

5.6   ISSUES ARISING

Understanding analysis work is not easy. Designers and developers of tools often have undeclared assumptions about what analysis work is, and these assumptions can easily become embedded in the tools, resulting in a rupture between the work at hand and the tools to accomplish the work.

Lucy Suchman demonstrated this clearly in her seminal work on the false cognitive assumptions that software developers can make that later cause very challenging problems for end users [191]. In her study the interface she studied was a complex photocopier's interface, and participants in her study were completely unable to finish moderately difficult and necessary tasks because of the way the interface was designed, and this was traced back to the popular, but erroneous, models of cognition of the developers who wrote the software for the photocopier.

This is where theory can help. It can support an exploration of analysis work because it helps researchers focus on important aspects of the work and make sense of it in a well-defined theoretical context. This can lead to important theory-driven innovations, as shown by the many examples in this section. Should the theory-driven innovations not prove able to help analysis or collaboration in the way expected, then the theory can be challenged, adapted, or more appropriate, alternate theories can be explored. Iteration is still necessary when solutions are explored, but theory-driven work, at least, comes from a position where assumptions about human behavior are explicit and can be tried, challenged or debated.

This brief review has shown that theories exist to aid understanding of individual analysis work. These theories of individual analysis are primarily based on cognitive theories. However, increasing amounts of data and larger and more complex analyses are pushing for collaborative analysis work. We reviewed several relevant theories of collaboration, but others are possible and a seasoned researcher takes a critical and flexible approach to the theories (and methods) they adopt. Appropriate theories for a given situation are dependent on the nature of the research or the design work being conducted. By providing examples of how these theories have been applied in research we have shown their effectiveness for augmenting understanding and also for developing tools to support analysts. Theories are essential guides for designing surface interfaces.

CHAPTER 6

The Development of Surface Applications

In domains where the technology infrastructure is rapidly changing, interaction design and software development are closely linked activities. In this chapter we first briefly review a few good approaches to the development process that address issues pertinent to surface applications for analysis work. We then discuss user interaction toolkits for development of surface applications, with an emphasis on open frameworks for large surfaces important for collaborative analysis work.

6.1 APPLICATION DEVELOPMENT PROCESSES

As we have seen in earlier sections, surface applications demand a paradigm shift with respect to interaction design. Clearly the topic of application development processes can fill an entire bookshelf, and so we cannot hope to address the whole domain. Instead we briefly touch on a few tips to raise awareness of ways to incorporate interaction design and empirical evaluation into the development cycle, in particular where they apply to enabling visual analysis, collaboration, and rapidly evolving requirements.

6.1.1 DESIGNING FOR VISUAL ANALYSIS

Data analysis is a domain where analysts have significant expertise, and where application domains often have well-established conventions. While there is much general knowledge about information visualization, it is nevertheless important for any software development effort to work closely with analysts in the relevant domain. For example, Conti [48] presents a development process in chapter 10 of his book *Security Data Visualization* that specifically addresses software development for visual analysis. The process combines the expertise of visualization experts, user experience specialists, security experts and software developers. It considers hardware issues, memory issues, usability issues, software architecture issues, and domain issues, and helps experts from multiple domains coordinate their work.

At the heart of Conti's work is the awareness that "By definition, humans are integral to the visualization system." In stating the obvious he admonishes teams to never lose sight of the human while solving computer challenges. This leads to an iterative user-centered design process:

1. **Focus on Users/Tasks**

   Understanding users' goals and the tasks they must perform to achieve them is an essential element of user-centered design. The first challenge in visual analysis is to capture tasks that users may have difficulty articulating, particularly when there are aspects of discovery in the task. The next challenge is to keep users engaged in the minutiae of a sometimes laborious design process. This can be difficult with expert users whose time is best spent on their real work. This usually means identifying or training appropriate proxy users who can take the place of actual domain experts for certain tasks.

2. **Perform Empirical Evaluation**

   Designs should be validated early, involving domain experts (or their proxies) and interaction design professionals. Use prototypes extensively, starting with low fidelity paper-based ones, and gather data to validate design assumptions. When moving beyond paper-based prototypes consider using development tools that will make it possible to reach a broad range of usability testers.

3. **Iterate**

   Solutions should be built incrementally, incorporating lessons learned from earlier analysis and evaluation phases.

6.1.2   DESIGNING FOR RAPIDLY EVOLVING REQUIREMENTS

Changing requirements will likely be a hallmark of surface application design and development, because there are so many unknowns. End users will only know what they want in an application as they begin to comprehend the possibilities. In the third edition of *Interaction Design* [167], Rogers et al. claim that *agile software development* [44] practices offer the most promising strategies to integrate design into the development process. They acknowledge the variety of distinct agile methodologies, but point out that these strategies share similar benefits in their use of early and regular user feedback, their ability to handle emergent requirements, and their ability to balance flexibility and structure in a project plan. In brief, the main phases of the interaction design process they describe are: 1. Establish Requirements, 2. Design Alternatives, 3. Prototype, and 4. Evaluate. Because design and development work for surfaces is so novel, and therefore more unpredictable, agile methods appear very suitable.

Rogers et al. also raise the issue of when to begin work on implementation activities, particularly when combining the efforts of designers, developers, and users/evaluators. The underlying issue is that the interaction design and the software development are *both* iterative processes. They suggest one way to maintain productivity among these groups is to interleave their activities in parallel tracks (Figure 6.1) in a manner described at Toronto-based Alias Systems (now owned by Autodesk) [192]. They call their iterations 'cycles.' In Cycle 0 the most important features are investigated and prioritized. In Cycle 1 the developers work on features requiring little design

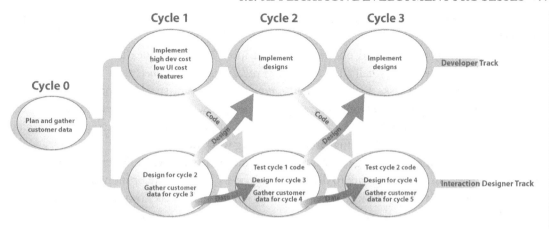

Figure 6.1: Interleaved parallel tracks in interaction design and development work. Source: based on *Journal of Usability Studies* [192]

input while interaction designers produce their initial designs and gather user data. In subsequent cycles the developers implement features designed in Cycle n-1 while interaction designers test code implemented in Cycle n-1, design features for Cycle n+1, and gather customer input for Cycle n+2. By interleaving the activities of designers, developers, and customers all three groups are able to maintain a high level of communications and productivity.

Agile methodologies gain several advantages from their user-centred focus, but perhaps the most powerful is the frequency of evaluation. It should be noted, however, that while user input is essential, users typically lack the formal background to fully evaluate prospective design solutions. Therefore, while it is essential to include users (or suitable proxies) in the establishment of requirements it is also important to apply due diligence with empirical and heuristic techniques. Examples of such techniques include: Wizard-of-Oz testing with low-fidelity prototypes that uncover issues as early as possible; cognitive walkthroughs that guide analysts through potentially challenging tasks with a focus on mental models; and heuristic evaluations that examine the overall product with respect to established dimensions of usability. These *discount* evaluation techniques are named for their low cost and their good rate of problem discovery, both features that increase the likelihood that they will be used in spite of schedule and budget constraints [145]. In novel design situations frequent evaluations are particularly important.

6.1.3 USABILITY ANALYSIS TECHNIQUES

Designing software for collaboration introduces an important new dimension that can complicate evaluation efforts. Pinelle, Gutwin and Greenberg [153] point out that traditional discount evaluation techniques (e.g., inspections, walkthroughs, and heuristic evaluations) successfully address *individual work*, however they fail to model usability aspects specific to *teamwork*. To this end, they offer a framework called *Collaboration Usability Analysis* (CUA) to address this essential distinction.

Pinelle et al. use standard observational and interview techniques in a real-world work setting to discover what they call the *mechanics of collaboration*. The *mechanics* that are captured include communication tasks such as *explicit communication* (e.g., speaking, pointing, drawing, etc.) and *information gathering* (e.g., basic awareness of others, changes to objects, eye gaze direction), and coordination tasks such as *shared access* (e.g., taking tools, occupying space, reserving resources), and *transfer* (e.g., handing-off or depositing work items).

Having an explicit language to capture these mechanics allows designers to model these in diagrammatic forms, taking care to distinguish *taskwork* (i.e., private or individual tasks) from *teamwork* (i.e., group-related tasks). They offer a diagram model of task flows with Boolean AND, OR, XOR paths, and they also capture branching and iteration. The goal is not to produce a fixed structure representing a proscribed group dynamic, but rather to capture the essence of each task and represent its value to group objectives. The model can then be used as a resource for evaluating proposed software designs using discount methods. The model may be able to clearly show that the new design is better in some specific way, such as by providing better shared access to resources, in comparison to the old design.

In certain cases there is value in very detailed analyses of user behavior. Examples include analyzing data mined from system logs, or capturing the detailed mechanisms of collaboration through detailed observations as mentioned above. An alternative approach is to use eye-tracking. The principle is that, often, where we are looking is where we are attending, and where we are attending is especially important in collaborative activities.

As mentioned in section 5.4.3, for conventional desktop computer systems, Human-Computer Interaction specialists have used eye-tracking to study what users are looking at while using the software. This helps researchers link gaze with the current state of a user's mind, and can provide insights into such things as distractions. This can be a useful technique during a usability study to determine how to improve layout and information architecture [126]. During usability tests a researcher could use eye-tracking to examine the amount of fixations or duration of fixations to discern objects of interest on a display. Alternately, Komogortsev et al. suggest that excessive eye scanning could imply a usability problem [112].

For collaborative systems, such as those with large surfaces or multiple devices, eye-tracking can also be useful. When individuals are co-located and communicating, both eye expressions and eye directions are components of interaction. For example, the direction of a pupil's gaze is often leveraged by teachers to ensure that students are attending to the proper material during a lesson. Head-mounted eye-trackers, such as the Tobii device shown earlier in figure 5.7, allow tracking of gaze around a large screen, between smaller devices, and beyond to the general environment.

We see eye movements and eye expressions as a part of a rich social interchange aimed at achieving a common ground between colaborators [40].

6.2   APPLICATION DEVELOPMENT FRAMEWORKS

The early 1980s brought the revolutionary Xerox Star interface [185]. Since then, personal computers and their operating systems have co-evolved to support the desktop GUI paradigm known as WIMP, an acronym for Windows, Icons, Menus and Pointers. While all these terms are pluralized by convention, the fact is that desktop systems support only one cursor pointer. In spite of multi-touch trackpads' appearance on Apple's MacBook Air in 2008, or PCs that support a mouse, a trackpad, and possibly even an isometric laptop joystick, all these controls actually refer to a singular cursor.

With the advent of the collaborative tabletop [141], the latest successor to the desktop and the laptop, we can now take the plural form 'Pointers' literally. This trivial grammatical observation represents a significant engineering challenge. The management of multiple simultaneous users around a single display has implications all the way from hardware detection to window design. In some ways it is the computer equivalent of installing multiple steering wheels on a car. Extending the automotive analogy a little further, operating systems are gradually improving their support for multiple simultaneous controls, but these are typically still in service of a single human driver. Support for multi-touch gestures is getting stronger, but the ability to distinguish one person's input from another's is typically outside the scope of today's operating system requirements. A number of system architects have understood the features essential to surface collaboration and new development tools and frameworks are emerging every year. The WIMP approach emerged about the same time as Object-Oriented Programming (OOP), and despite framework design diversity that continues to this day, there was symbiotic relationship between WIMP and OOP that facilitated some consensus. In surface computing there is little sign so far of anything similar.

Our own research has led us to focus on the development of applications on large surface displays with tangential forays into application development on handheld Android devices. This is a rather narrower developer focus than the broader scope illustrated by the many examples in this book, but we hope that its apparent confinement will seem a reasonable and pragmatic compromise. In keeping with the NUI focus alluded to in the introduction of chapter 3, we discuss the subset of surface technologies that have offered our team opportunities to move beyond the WIMP paradigm. In short, when *talking tech* we prefer to focus on tools we've seen first hand.

6.2.1   FEATURES OF MULTI-TOUCH DEVELOPMENT FRAMEWORKS

Enabling surface interaction requires more effort than simply running applications designed for the mouse on hardware capable of detecting touches. Such applications do not take advantage of multi-touch capabilities, are not sensitive to gestures and do not support collaboration well.

In our work we have used a number of multi-touch frameworks. We have had a preference for cross-platform support because it enables our team members and users to work with platforms they are already using. In practice, cross-platform support has also meant open-source frameworks because there are no cross-platform proprietary frameworks. An advantage of open source is that multi-touch is still evolving, and wider input helps to be able to advance the state of the art.

Frameworks that we used for any duration were chosen for their focus on surface collaboration, and for the maturity of their framework. We have come to see the following features as essential to the creation of multi-touch multi-user surface applications.

1. **Tabletop Canvas**

   Multi-touch tabletop interfaces are based on a drawing metaphor typically known as a canvas. The canvas takes the place of an operating system desktop—the standard WIMP design—and introduces support for rotation and resizing along with new multi-cursor modes of input. The canvas is automatically repainted many times per second, generating the perception of an animated surface.

2. **TUIO input provider**

   For applications that require touch events from devices across a port (or if touch events need to be passed across the network) there is a transport layer communication protocol for touch and motion data called TUIO [102]. Riding on a network protocol called Open Sound Control [43] originally designed for transmitting events from musical synthesizers and other multimedia devices, the TUIO protocol has become the de-facto standard for sharing multi-touch cursor events from a number of different event sources.

   One important advantage of using a network protocol to send touch information is the ability to forward touches to another machine. This helps enable very large displays to be built from arrays of smaller ones (Figure 6.2).

Figure 6.2: Large multi-touch, multi-person displays. Source: `http://multitouch.fi`

3. **Ability to define and incorporate new input providers**

The provision for new input sources, such as Microsoft Kinect devices or real-time networked collaborators, enables new modes of interaction. There are also other proprietary drivers for receiving gestural input from camera images or from accelerometers. Sometimes touch events will be transmitted through the operating system or indirectly through browser applications. In general it must be possible to define and configure the varied sources of touch events to applications.

4. **Touch optimized UI elements with support for rotation and resizing**

User interface widgets must support rotating and resizing so they can be used comfortably on all sides of a tabletop system and with a reasonably large number of collaborators. Ideally it should be possible to change their visual style based on tags or descriptors such as we find in HTML with CSS. The inclusion of layout managers for grouped UI elements is also helpful. Widgets must also support high resolution text elements.

5. **Gesture definition, localization and prioritization**

Definition and recognition of custom multi-touch gestures presents several challenges. In essence, sets of otherwise independent events must be interpreted as joint events. Gesture points must be grouped when they are within a reasonably small range of each other, allowing multiple simultaneous users to perform multi-touch gestures independently. In the event that a given touch is ambiguous, for instance if it falls inside the range of more than one gesture, then the system must be able to prioritize its assignment to a specific gesture according to an appropriate set of rules. This calls for the definition of ad-hoc "cursor collections" that map each cursor to exactly one gesture.

6. **Graphics and multimedia**

Multi-touch frameworks can be measured by the extent to which their API reduces the complexity of encoding interactive graphics. The necessary simplification of an API can sometimes limit outlying cases, and so some access to the underlying hardware accelerated graphics library (i.e., OpenGL) can also be useful. Multimedia hooks are also useful for creating mashups with rich streaming content.

7. **Flexible Event-Based Architecture**

Events in multi-touch applications can have much more nuance than the pointer-based idiom of traditional GUI frameworks. It is important to be able to react to events raised by partially completed gestures, off-target or out-of-bounds gestures, gesture timer expirations, and so on.

The next set of features may not be essential but they are certainly nice to have.

1. **Layout Language**

   An extensible language for application definition can greatly improve maintainability.

2. **Multiple virtual keyboards**

   Multiple users should be able to enter text independently into their own separate windows.

3. **Multiple cursor pools**

   It should be possible to group cursors according to their source. For instance it should be possible to distinguish between remote cursors and local ones, and it should be possible to distinguish between pen input and mice or touch points. These distinctions are not necessary for simple operations, but they are quite useful for providing gesture processing with important collaborative dimensions such as a participant's identity.

4. **Plugin gesture processing**

   Gesture interpretation can be achieved a number of ways. Most frameworks will have some sort of predefined gesture engine, but ideally it should be possible to use custom engines that use techniques such as rule-based processing or machine learning.

5. **Physics Library**

   Simulated physics adds a measure of realism to multi-touch interfaces. Some elements of this approach were explored early, such as the inertial scrolling seen in the experimental Star7 personal digital assistant demonstrated in 1992. This has now become a commonplace feature, especially in smartphones and tablet. The idea is to provide an experience that better matchs the experience of an actual control wheel for scrolling documents and lists. The more general appeal of simulated physics has been shown in experiments for drag and drop on the desktop [1], and being actively explored for multi-touch interfaces.

6.2.2   OS-SPECIFIC FRAMEWORKS

Some platforms represent end-to-end designs that include native tools. Examples of this include SMART Technologies' SMART API, MultiTouch Ltd.'s Cornerstone SDK, Google's Android SDK, Apple's UIKit framework, and Microsoft's Surface 2.0 SDK. When working with such hardware the advantage of commercial tools is often worth the expense. Software features are well-matched with hardware capabilities, and documentation and support are often available.

Microsoft created a broad set of tools for their Surface 2.0 hardware, and the same tools applied when the Surface brand was re-assigned from their large multi-touch table to their tablet. The Surface 2.0 software development kit (SDK) extends the Windows Presentation Foundation (WPF) to provide the essentials of redesigned UI elements, multi-user support, etc., that we identified in section 6.2.1. For example, the producers of the Surface SDK understood the need to redesign their interface elements (buttons, sliders, text boxes, containers, etc.) given the new challenges of surface interaction.

In some frameworks with native OS integration, such as the Qt Framework [147], we find a more gradual transition from a strictly WIMP paradigm to a mix of WIMP and multi-touch support. In modifying existing interface elements the result is a mix of interaction paradigms that presents implementation challenges for developers, who must carefully choose from a growing set of widget features to produce an appropriate effect in the appropriate context. By contrast, Nuiteq's Snowflake Suite [149] is an example of a commercial framework designed from the ground up with multi-touch in mind.

6.2.3   PYTHON-BASED FRAMEWORKS

In our work we have focused on development environments that promise cross-platform support and rapid prototyping of multi-touch applications. The Python language Kivy library and its predecessor PyMT are examples of frameworks designed for rapid development of multi-touch applications. They support all our essential requirements and some of the others we considered desirable. Both projects are open-source projects.

Kivy has an active developer community with a demonstrated commitment to cross-platform development with initial input support for Windows, Mac OSX and Linux, and more recently with additional support for Android and iOS. Our experience with its predecessor PyMT (under Windows and Linux) confirmed our hope that it was possible to rapidly design prototypes with good performance and a polished look and feel. The Kivy graphics support engines provide a simplified API for newcomers to graphics programming. The expandable design made it possible to plug in new input sources and libraries for rendering charts and graphs.

PyMT came with a number of core UI widgets that could be easily rotated and resized for use on tabletop systems. They also provided a simplified class that could inherit these abilities, enabling the design of customized UI elements. A useful range of example projects were provided to augment PyMT's somewhat sparse documentation. Having established a presence with PyMT in the multi-touch community, the developers of the Kivy project appear to be better funded. Issues such as its initially sparse documentation are now rapidly being addressed.

The architecture of Kivy (Figure 6.3) includes support (lower left) for the external libraries typically used for images, text, audio, and video. Graphics (lower center) are rendered with hardware-acceleration implemented in C for performance. Support for many multi-touch input devices for different operating systems (lower right) is built in. The core providers section in the middle layer shows support for windowing, text (spell checking can be included), image loading, audio, and video. Many of an application's low-level details can be customized by configuration in the core provider section, permitting output using a 2D engine of your choice, such as pygame or SDL. The middle layer also contains API abstractions for OpenGL, offering access to advanced visualizations. The input abstractions allow for de-jittering and post-processing, and also serve as examples of simple event processing. For most applications the defaults in the lower and middle layers require no adjustment, however it is noteworthy that modifications at this level are relatively easy to achieve given Kivy's Python roots.

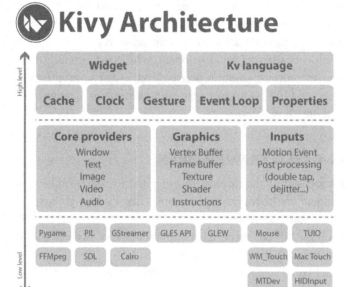

Figure 6.3: A platform for rapid cross-platform multi-touch applications. The Kivy Architecture. Source: based on kivy.org

The top layer of Kivy's architecture is the one most developers will interact with, as this includes the application abstractions. The major distinction that the Kivy developers introduced after PyMT was the invention of the Kivy language, a set of declarative constructs meant to describe user interfaces and interactions. This definitional language will offer a critical foundation for potential visual designers of the kind we see exploited in more commercially supported architectures like Microsoft's WPF or Java Swing.

In addition to Kivy and PyMT, we must also mention another Python-based library, also with a declarative model at its core. This more mature library is called *libavg* [212]. Written in C++ for performance, the libavg project has been in active development since 2003 and uses Python as a scripting language to develop interactive media applications. While our team has not had experience coding with this framework, it is notable for its use in engaging public exhibits, multi-user games, educational maps [213], and medical simulators. Libavg runs on Linux, Mac OS X, and Windows.

6.2.4   JAVA-BASED FRAMEWORKS

Written in the Java language, the MT4j Framework [118] offers a favorable mix of architectural layers, UI components, performance, maturity, and extensibility. MT4j uses a language called *Processing* [68] as its application container and as an animated canvas. Everything from GUI elements to touch keyboards are rendered by and listened to through this environment, and the event loop of Processing's PApplet is the heartbeat of an MT4j application.

The Java-based language *Processing* and its development environment were originally developed as tools for teaching computer programming to students, artists, designers, researchers, and anybody interested in doing computational work in a visual context. Processing runs on numerous platforms and has access to a great variety of libraries including (but not limited to) animation, 3D rendering, sound and video processing, networking, physics simulation, and numerous data import and export utilities.

At first glance, Processing can seem like a toy language (Figure 6.4(a)) but its apparent simplicity has made it attractive to interaction designers in several domains from network intrusion visualization to realtime geographic visualizations of telecom data (Figure 6.4(b)).

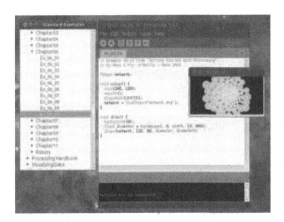

(a) Simple Example Source: [162]   (b) Advanced Example. Source: [115]

Figure 6.4: Examples of visualization applications produced with Processing.

MT4j essentially extends Processing to support the essentials of tabletop interaction. It contains gesture definition tools, a physics engine, several sample applications, and reasonably good documentation. The project is still in pre-release status while the authors incorporate support for the Android operating system and finalize their roadmap.

The architectural layers for the desktop package of MT4J are shown in Figure 6.5 (note that in this case the term 'desktop' distinguishes it from Android packaging; the actual surface could be a full wall or a large table display). As in the case with the Kivy diagram, the architecture is presented by the authors of the framework. Their focus in this diagram is somewhat different from that of Kivy. There are fewer options shown in the lower layers, and the middle layers explain the abstraction of events from the hardware layer. This reflects the somewhat more rigid design of MT4J, with low and middle layer decisions defined to support the rendering layer at the top right of the stack (Kivy lets you choose renderers appropriate to your platform). Note

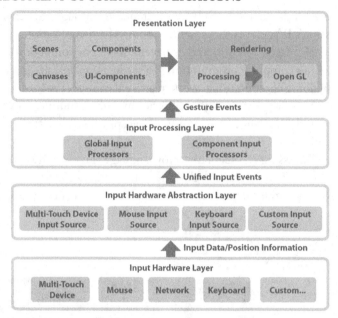

Figure 6.5: Multi-touch application MT4j architecture. Source: based on mt4j.org

that the box called 'Processing' refers to the language and not a computational activity. A useful set of abstractions in MT4J that are somewhat less obvious in Kivy's diagram are the Scene and Component abstractions in the upper left of the presentation layer. These represent windowing abstractions, and the documentation for their use is quite good.

One aspect of MT4J's architecture that isn't clear from the diagram is the fact that the Processing language has a number of open source libraries of its own that developers might employ for a variety of input and output extensions. For instance MT4J comes with excellent demo programs including particle physics, 3D graphics, rich gestures, world maps, and many others.

6.2.5   WEB-BASED FRAMEWORKS

Recent advances in web browser design have raised interest in the web as a target platform for multi-touch. Visualizations have improved with the emergence of the HTML5 canvas, the broader adoption of SVG, and the 3D potential of WebGL. Realtime communications have improved with the advent of WebSockets and WebRTC (Real-Time Communications). Performance has improved with advances in JavaScript compilation. Taken together these advances in browser design should make it possible to produce rich interactive and collaborative graphical interfaces for great varieties of user surfaces, from tabletops and desktops to tablets and smartphones.

The advantages of web deployment are that one application can be run on any platform, and without any need to explicitly install or update. The disadvantages are limited access to local sensors or resources, but those same limitations are also beneficial for security. The basic idea is to leverage web browsers as standards-based development platforms, and improvements in browser performance and capability make this increasingly attractive. It must be mentioned, however, that browser implementations are not entirely uniform. The touch specification for HTML is still evolving, and browser compliances vary. We find a proliferation of client-side JavaScript libraries for each of the major architectural components outlined in previous sections, and many of these are excellent. But still there hasn't been a single reference web framework for multi-touch that includes *all* the important pieces, at least not yet.

In the past it might have been worth considering Adobe Flash as a potential development platform for web-enabled rich user interfaces capable of touch, but with Apple refusing to support Flash on iOS, with Adobe's recent announcement that after version 11.2 they will be discontinuing their standalone player for Linux (current plans are to make it available only as a plugin for Google Chrome), and with Microsoft's move in Windows 8 toward a "plugin-free" version of Internet Explorer, but at this point HTML5 and JavaScript have more cross-platform merit.

Moving away from Flash we find no shortage of pure JavaScript visualization toolkits that are great candidates for web-based surface interaction. The Processing language used by MT4J has been ported to JavaScript [69], and with the addition of touch (in release 1.1) it is now possible to reproduce something like MT4j's interaction capabilities in canvas-capable web browsers. The D3 library [26, 27], Raphaël [13], and KineticJS [107], also handle touch events.

Choosing a framework may depend on your application and any legacy browsers you may need to support. Processing.js and KineticJS are both based on the HTML5 Canvas, while Raphaël and D3 manipulate SVG images (note: Raphaël quietly produces VML images for older versions of MSIE). Canvas-based images may be quicker to animate, particularly when adding or removing large numbers of distinct elements. SVG-based images may be easier to manipulate and they scale exceptionally well.

While the SVG protocol has been specified for some time, it has only recently begun to have a broad impact. Better built-in browser support is one reason, and now more usable JavaScript libraries, such as Raphaël and D3, are gaining widespread use in visualization applications. Ironically, the inclusion of the raster-based HTML5 Canvas appears to have drawn attention to the vector-based SVG as a useful alternative more suitable for applications requiring scalability. The lack of support for Adobe Flash in many mobile devices may also be a factor.

One of the challenges to overcome when dealing with multi-touch is the need to unify gesture processing across multiple computing platforms. Each of the major operating systems—particularly in handheld devices—has its own methods for producing and handling advanced gestural events, and browsers themselves have differences in how they consume these events. Work is under way by producers of open source JavaScript libraries to simplify this situation and offer a common gestural vocabulary [201].

Another design question worth exploring is whether the handheld experience of a given web application should *mirror* or *complement* the desktop or tabletop experience. In our own early explorations we have found advantages in treating these as complementary use cases, even in the context of real time collaboration. For instance in a prototype Agile cardwall application we found that text input was best achieved with personal devices while a more global rendering of the wall was presented to users of large surface tabletops or wall-mounted displays. Handheld devices also offered opportunities to distinguish between private off-line and public real-time interaction with shared visualizations (i.e., touch points can be contained locally or shared globally). Finally, the ability to distinguish the identity of a handheld device user presents an opportunity for authorization and tracking of changes to shared application state. These distinctions have important implications for framework design.

The prototype architecture (Figure 6.6) we developed for our first agile cardwall prototype has multi-touch capability and an animated view for collaborators updated in near real-time over the web. With a careful choice of JavaScript libraries and server configuration we were able to demonstrate collaboration across browsers running on Windows, Linux, OS/X, iOS, and Android operating systems. However, our system lacks the advanced features of more mature desktop multi-touch frameworks (such as advanced gestures). The relative lack of client-side features compared with Kivy and MT4J reflects an early stage of development for web-based multi-touch applications. Ultimately there will be JavaScript analogues for many of the components in these more mature frameworks.

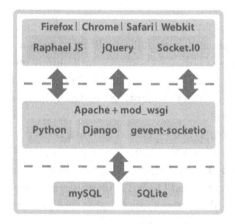

Figure 6.6: Web multi-touch application architecture.

This web architecture diagram (Figure 6.6) serves a different purpose than those of the desktop architectures. In this case we show a browser-based client-server architecture supporting desktop and handheld browsers, and we call attention to the bidirectional communication using web sockets. This offers the web application an opportunity to update a shared model for collaboration. Note that the ability to share a display across the web brings with it a risk that latency will affect shared application state. With multiple users potentially contributing multiple cursors (or touch-points), questions can arise as to which input events to process, how to present interim or provisional states, and what to do when conflicting updates occur. Other new web capabilities may also play a role. For example WebRTC (Web Real-Time Communication) may be useful for media transfer. Our more recent architectures are being designed to explore these questions more fully and we look forward to reporting our results. Some of the issues are presented in the multi-surface section 6.3.

6.2.6   CHOOSING A FRAMEWORK

How you choose between the different possible toolkits will depend on a number of factors. Issues include your experience with programming languages, your comfort with image manipulation, the availability of touch-based hardware for development (perhaps needing less expensive simulation) and release (potentially targeting a variety of mass market devices), the range of platforms you need to target, and the need to incorporate novel modes of interaction.

Many of the open source toolkits are rapidly evolving projects with open issues on the various operating systems they support. You may find that your new idea for multi-modal interaction violates a number of assumptions that span an entire open source architectural stack. This could be seen as a barrier to research, but it can also be seen as an opportunity to improve an open source toolkit or even as an opportunity to research and derive your own tools.

In the large display and mixed-surface environments—our own current focus—we find that the Python-based and browser-based environments are a good fit. For developers without access to a large touch surface, Kivy can simulate touches with a mouse or touchpad. Kivy developers have also targeted the broadest range of surface platforms, from large custom-built displays to smaller iOS and Android devices.

The browser-based tools are an ongoing development challenge but we see great potential in its near-instantaneous deployment and its use in remote collaboration with small and large surfaces. Our latest project employs node.js [91] as a web server, a collaboration server, and a TUIO interpreter, and we are working on client-side JavaScript to encode a gesture processing layer using a state-machine model. We tend to choose SVG-based visualization toolkits for the advantage they bring in designing interfaces. It is possible to sketch a visualization in Inkscape, export the resulting SVG code, and then bring it to life with Raphaël or D3 [208]. Detailed JavaScript debugging is made possible even in remote handheld devices with the advent of remote web inspector tools [139].

Developers familiar with Java may prefer MT4J and possibly Android, both of which can be developed entirely within the Eclipse IDE. We have used both toolkits to experiment with mixed-surface gestures. The richness of visualizations available in Processing combined with MT4J's use of OpenGL and physics can produce stunning results. Their fluid dynamics sample gets a lot of attention at demo days in the lab. Working with the Android SDK offers developers a good simulation platform as well as very rapid deployment to actual USB-attached devices. It is even possible to embed a browser *within* an Android application, offering the combined benefits of web-based and native code.

Many people work within a Microsoft environment for development and deployment, and use tools based on Microsoft's .NET Framework. For instance, a research framework for "proxemic interaction" at the University of Calgary [128] is published as an open source .NET library. Also Microsoft's *Expression Blend* and *Expression Web* designers have been designed to work with the Surface 2.0 SDK. Designers can find numerous videos explaining how to use these commercial tools to produce professional designs for Windows-based systems.

6.3   ISSUES ARISING

To conclude we summarize issues that arise when selecting multi-touch frameworks to enable multi-surface collaboration (collaboration that is enabled by multiple surfaces).

Few multi-touch surfaces have the means to identify the source of gestures when several collaborators are interacting with a single screen. Some notable exceptions are the Diamond-Touch [55] table which identifies users by means of capacitive charges in their chairs, or systems designed around Anoto digital pens which have unique Bluetooth identifiers. Other techniques have been suggested using a variety of heuristics, such as differences in territory, skin tone, or behavior. However, the ubiquity and low cost of tablets and smartphones offers a excellent opportunity to provide the identiy of collaborators, as well as additional modes of interaction beyond touch. Further, tablets and smartphones as additional devices for collaboration can offer opportunities for private exploration, offline data manipulation and preparation, and interactions requiring personalization or authority.

The technologies mentioned in the previous section, particularly web-based frameworks, are a good starting point for collaborating across multiple devices. However, there remain differences in how gestures are shared with browsers within each of the main handheld operating systems, and so it may be worth designing for a mix of browser-based and native code.

Prior to exploring browser-based technologies we experimented with multi-screen approaches using MT4J and PyMT. Our early designs were based on simply sharing TUIO touch events across multiple collaborating systems, and we quickly discovered a number of challenges in this space. These challenges were, briefly:

- a shortage of published research in the domain of simultaneous multi-device multi-touch input

- a lack of research on gesture interpretation in the context of collaborating devices

- system and protocol implementations that assumed only single-system sources of touch

Multi-device touch input was a peripheral component of our larger projects and while we did proceed to solve the essential implementation issues with MT4J there remained a number of challenges to be addressed. The shortage of published research was addressed in a paper published months later by Liu, Feng, and Li [125] that presents networking protocols and algorithms that ensure responsive and error-free streaming of multi-touch events between networked devices.

Additional work is still required in the social aspects of this component of collaboration. Our own experiences did manage to generate some potentially useful insights. We offer the following observations:

1. Remote cursors are very useful for collaboration, however they should probably be for display only on remote machines. Multi-touch gestures should generally ignore remote cursor sources.

2. In the event that an event requires multiple collaborators, for instance in a voting scenario or in cases where more than one participant is required for authority, then alternative schemes can be devised that make use of shared system state.

3. The challenge of sharing application state across multiple devices gives rise to an important question of the identity of objects. It is important to draw appropriate distinctions between actual objects and inferred or proxy objects. Mutability (the ability of objects to be changed) of shared objects must follow logic that meets mutually shared goals of participants.

4. Remote manipulation of shared visual artifacts can create conflicting events. Depending on system latency, remote users may consistently have their updates rolled back. All displays should quickly reflect provisional changes to shared state.

5. Display of shared state on client devices may represent an aggregation based on large amounts of underlying data, however it is impractical for each device to keep local copies of each of these underlying objects. Care must be taken to provide enough copied data for responsive local manipulation but not so much that its maintenance becomes a performance burden.

6. Additional performance cost on small devices can come from the container classes used to render objects on screen. This is particularly evident when displays use simulated physics for animated realism. Since the screen itself is physically limited this forms a natural opportunity to improve performance by reusing existing containers that have scrolled outside the display area rather than recreating them as manipulation demands.

CHAPTER 7

Concluding Comments

Our review of the use of surface technologies for collaborative work summarized the most recent literature and then identified issues that suggest gaps and challenges for future research. We reviewed issues to do with technology, both hardware and software, making the point that this area is developing very rapidly. We also emphasized that large multi-touch surfaces of various types are increasingly affordable, and that many researchers have seen this type of technology as being particularly suited to enabling collaborative work.

Our discussion of hardware and software informed our discussion about designing for collaborative work using large interactive surfaces and mixed-display environments. We are very optimistic about surface computing, and our purpose here was to provide a foundation to encourage engagement in the challenging social, theoretical, experiential and computational problems that arise as a result of the introduction of surface technologies.

Although there are many collaborative work activities, we addressed the changing nature of analysis work in particular. Analysis work is in general becoming more collaborative, more multidisciplinary, and increasingly involves larger and larger amounts of complex data (in extreme cases, this is called 'big data'). Large surfaces in mixed-display environments seem well poised to support this new form of activity. Within the broader context of collaborative analysis work we particularly discussed analysis work in the security domain which is typically either network security or intelligence work. We emphasize the development of this work, but we intend our discussion of analysis work in the security domain as an example of the evolving nature of analysis work in general. There are many other types of analysis work that are also collaborative.

To conclude, we briefly detail the insights that we have derived as a result of our literature review and our work with our industry partners who are eager to adopt surface technologies.

Design for surface applications in the analysis domain requires a system perspective. Surface computing is only as useful as its application software, and applications for collaborative analysis work need carefully designed interfaces and software. Further, surface computing environments need appropriate accommodation and infrastructure, which also needs to be designed. In this context it is important to design with an eye to end-user interaction, end-user experiences, and the broader environment, which would include team interactions and the physical aspects of the workplace.

Design for surface applications requires an understanding of the challenging aspects of collaborative work, especially in the context of larger data sets. New information visualization and interaction formalisms that take advantage of higher resolution surfaces need to be developed. Further mixed-display environments (surface and non-surface) supporting both team and individual work will become increasingly important. Well-designed environments also need to support the natural flow of work artifacts between displays.

Interaction design for surface computing presents novel challenges that are not easily solved by mechanisms used for traditional desktop interaction design. Menus and scrollbars may become things of the past, and new approaches to pointing, selecting, and hovering are required. Gesturing is the emerging approach, and is still evolving. Easy text entry and interactor identity remain challenges.

Theory can be a valuable tool in providing overall direction to design work. Collaborative artifact-mediated work can be understood from a variety of theoretical perspectives. However, collaborative work, such as collaborative analysis work can be especially challenging to understand and predict, particularly where new technology presents unfamiliar opportunities. Ongoing research on the suitability and applicability of various theoretical approaches is needed to best inform the design of surface computing environments for collaborative analysis work.

With respect to software architecture and development there is and will continue to be some turbulence as technology standards and design best practices emerge and become established. It is very important for designers to understand this, as the challenges for developers are much greater than in WIMP (windows, icons, menus and pointer) interfaces. Diversity of toolkits and libraries may make cross-platform development problematic until the advantages of interoperability influence the market. Similarly, heterogeneity of data sources and formats may present challenges. Expertise in development tools and interaction design skills for surfaces will initially be rare. We described the issues faced by software developers at a high level to help to clarify the challenges of surface projects that aim to support collaboration.

Surface computing is likely to become commonplace in some domains such as entertainment, education and social data analysis. However, we also expect large surfaces will serve a primary role in supporting collaborative work. Meeting rooms and team environments will be designed to feature large surfaces. These large surfaces, while being a key to enabling more collaborative computing environments, will typically work in concert with other display devices in mixed-display environments, where both individual and team devices are used together to support collaborative work. We believe large displays and mixed display environments (combinations of large displays, tablets, smartphones and other types of surfaces) will become ubiquitous in office environments of the future. In this emerging and novel context, application software, and especially application interfaces, must be explicitly and purposefully designed and developed to support surface computing for collaborative work. This book described current research in this space, and provided a perspective on it based on our own experiences and expertise.

Bibliography

[1] Anand Agarawala and Ravin Balakrishnan. Keepin' it real: pushing the desktop metaphor with physics, piles and the pen. In *Proceedings of the SIGCHI conference on Human Factors in computing systems*, CHI '06, pages 1283–1292, New York, NY, 2006. ACM. DOI: 10.1145/1124772.1124965 104

[2] Christopher Ahlberg and Ben Shneiderman. Visual information seeking: Tight coupling of dynamic query filters with starfield displays. In *Proceedings of the SIGCHI Conference on Human Factors in Computing Systems*, CHI '94, pages 313–317, New York, NY, USA, 1994. ACM. DOI: 10.1145/191666.191775 74

[3] R.A. Amar and J.T. Stasko. Knowledge precepts for design and evaluation of information visualizations. *IEEE Transactions on Visualization and Computer Graphics*, 11(4):432–442, Jul.-Aug. 2005. DOI: 10.1109/TVCG.2005.63 74, 76

[4] Christopher Andrews, Alex Endert, and Chris North. Space to think: Large high-resolution displays for sensemaking. In *Proceedings of the 28th international conference on Human factors in computing systems*, CHI '10, pages 55–64, New York, NY, 2010. ACM. DOI: 10.1145/1753326.1753336 53, 54

[5] Caroline Appert, Olivier Chapuis, and Emmanuel Pietriga. High-precision magnification lenses. In *Proceedings of the 28th international conference on Human factors in computing systems*, CHI '10, pages 273–282, New York, NY, 2010. ACM. DOI: 10.1145/1753326.1753366 36

[6] Stefan Bachl, Martin Tomitsch, Karin Kappel, and Thomas Grechenig. The effects of personal displays and transfer techniques on collaboration strategies in multi-touch based multi-display environments. In *Proceedings of the 13th IFIP TC 13 international conference on Human-computer interaction - Volume Part III*, INTERACT'11, pages 373–390, Berlin, Heidelberg, 2011. Springer-Verlag. DOI: 10.1007/978-3-642-23765-2_26 62, 63, 65

[7] Aruna D. Balakrishnan. Sensemaking with shared visualizations: Investigating the effects of visualizations in remote collaborative analysis. Technical report, Carnegie Mellon University, August 2011. Available at http://reports-archive.adm.cs.cmu.edu/anon/hcii/CMU-HCII-11-104.pdf. 59

[8] Aruna D. Balakrishnan, Susan R. Fussell, and Sara Kiesler. Do visualizations improve synchronous remote collaboration? In *Proceedings of the twenty-sixth annual SIGCHI conference*

on Human factors in computing systems, CHI '08, pages 1227–1236, New York, NY, 2008. ACM. DOI: 10.1145/1357054.1357246 59

[9] Aruna D. Balakrishnan, Susan R. Fussell, Sara Kiesler, and Aniket Kittur. Pitfalls of information access with visualizations in remote collaborative analysis. In *Proceedings of the 2010 ACM conference on Computer supported cooperative work*, CSCW '10, pages 411–420, New York, NY, 2010. ACM. DOI: 10.1145/1718918.1718988 59

[10] Robert Ball and Chris North. An analysis of user behavior on high-resolution tiled displays. In *Proceedings of the 2005 IFIP TC13 international conference on Human-Computer Interaction*, INTERACT'05, pages 350–363, Berlin, Heidelberg, 2005. Springer-Verlag. DOI: 10.1007/11555261_30 52, 53

[11] Robert Ball and Chris North. Effects of tiled high-resolution display on basic visualization and navigation tasks. In *CHI '05 extended abstracts on Human factors in computing systems*, CHI EA '05, pages 1196–1199, New York, NY, 2005. ACM. DOI: 10.1145/1056808.1056875 52

[12] Amartya Banerjee, Jesse Burstyn, Audrey Girouard, and Roel Vertegaal. Pointable: An in-air pointing technique to manipulate out-of-reach targets on tabletops. In *Proceedings of the ACM international conference on Interactive tabletops and surfaces*, ITS '11, pages 11–20, New York, NY, 2011. ACM. DOI: 10.1145/2076354.2076357 35

[13] Dmitry Baranovskiy. Raphaël. Available at: `http://raphaeljs.com/`. 109

[14] Benjamin B. Bederson and Ben Shneiderman, editors. *The Craft of Information Visualization*. Morgan Kaufmann Publishers, San Francisco, CA, 2003. 75

[15] Benjamin B. Bederson, Ben Shneiderman, and Martin Wattenberg. Ordered and quantum treemaps: Making effective use of 2D space to display hierarchies. *ACM Transactions on Graphics*, 21(4):833–854, October 2002. DOI: 10.1145/571647.571649 75

[16] Hrvoje Benko, Andrew D. Wilson, and Patrick Baudisch. Precise selection techniques for multi-touch screens. In *Proceedings of the SIGCHI conference on Human Factors in computing systems*, CHI '06, pages 1263–1272, New York, NY, 2006. ACM. DOI: 10.1145/1124772.1124963 42, 43

[17] Nick Berggren, Ernst H. W. Koster, and Nazanin Derakshan. The effect of cognitive load in emotional attention and trait anxiety: An eye movement study. *Journal of Cognitive Psychology*, 24(1):79–91, 2012. DOI: 10.1080/20445911.2011.618450 85

[18] Olav W Bertelsen and S. Bødker. Activity theory. In J.M. Carroll, editor, *HCI models, theories, and frameworks: Toward a multidisciplinary science*, chapter 11, pages 291–324. Morgan Kaufmann, San Francisco, CA, 2003. 94

[19] Daniel M. Best, Shawn Bohn, Douglas Love, Adam Wynne, and William A. Pike. Real-time visualization of network behaviors for situational awareness. In *Proceedings of the Seventh International Symposium on Visualization for Cyber Security*, VizSec '10, pages 79–90, New York, NY, 2010. ACM. DOI: 10.1145/1850795.1850805 17, 19

[20] Mark A. Beyer and David W. Cearley. *'Big Data' and content will challenge IT across the board.* Gartner Inc., 2012. 3

[21] Jacob T. Biehl, William T. Baker, Brian P. Bailey, Desney S. Tan, Kori M. Inkpen, and Mary Czerwinski. Impromptu: A new interaction framework for supporting collaboration in multiple display environments and its field evaluation for co-located software development. In *Proceedings of the twenty-sixth annual SIGCHI conference on Human factors in computing systems*, CHI '08, pages 939–948, New York, NY, 2008. ACM. DOI: 10.1145/1357054.1357200 62, 63

[22] Eric A. Bier, Maureen C. Stone, Ken Pier, William Buxton, and Tony D. DeRose. Toolglass and magic lenses: The see-through interface. In *Proceedings of the 20th annual conference on Computer graphics and interactive techniques*, SIGGRAPH '93, pages 73–80, New York, NY, 1993. ACM. DOI: 10.1145/166117.166126 36

[23] S. Bødker. *Through the interface: A human activity approach to user interface design.* CRC Press, 1990. 93

[24] Cheryl A. Bolstad and Mica R. Endsley. The effects of task load and shared displays on team situation awareness. In *Air Force Research Laboratory Report AFRL-HE-TR-1999-0243*, 1999. DOI: 10.1177/154193120004400150 57, 64

[25] Cheryl A. Bolstad, M. Riley Jennifer, Debra G. Jones, and Mica R. Endsley. Using goal directed task analysis with army brigade officer teams. In *Proceedings of the Human Factors and Ergonomics Society Annual Meeting*, volume 46, pages 472–476, 2002. DOI: 10.1177/154193120204600354 57

[26] Michael Bostock. D3.js. Available at: `http://d3js.org/`. 109

[27] Michael Bostock, Vadim Ogievetsky, and Jeffrey Heer. D3: Data-driven documents. *IEEE Trans. Visualization & Comp. Graphics (Proc. InfoVis)*, 2011. DOI: 10.1109/TVCG.2011.185 109

[28] Lauren Bradel, Christopher Andrews, Alex Endert, Katherine Vogt, Duke Hutchings, and Chris North. Space for two to think: Large, high-resolution displays for co-located collaborative sensemaking. Technical Report TR-11-11, Computer Science, Virginia Tech, 2011. 18, 22

[29] Judith Brown, Robert Biddle, and Steve Greenspan. Complex activities in an Operations Center: A case study and model for enginering interaction. In *Proceedings of the ACM 2009 international conference on Engineering Interactive Computer Systems*, EICS '13, New York, NY, 2013. ACM. 16

[30] Judith Brown, Stephen Greenspan, and Robert Biddle. Complex activities in an operations center: A case study and model for engineering interaction. In *Proceedings of ACM EICS 2009 Conference on Engineering Interactive Computing Systems*, EICS '13, New York, NY, 2013. ACM. DOI: 10.1145/2480296.2480310 92

[31] Judith M. Brown, Gitte Lindgaard, and Robert Biddle. Interactional identity: Designers and developers making joint work meaningful and effective. In *Proceedings of the ACM 2012 conference on Computer Supported Cooperative Work*, CSCW '12, pages 1381–1390, New York, NY, 2012. ACM. DOI: 10.1145/2145204.2145409 91

[32] Jeffrey Browne, Bongshin Lee, Sheelagh Carpendale, Nathalie Riche, and Timothy Sherwood. Data analysis on interactive whiteboards through sketch-based interaction. In *Proceedings of the ACM international conference on Interactive tabletops and surfaces*, ITS '11, pages 154–157, New York, NY, 2011. ACM. DOI: 10.1145/2076354.2076383 24, 26

[33] Aaron Bryden, George N. Phillips, Jr., Yoram Griguer, Jordan Moxon, and Michael Gleicher. Improving collaborative visualization of structural biology. In *Proceedings of the 7th international conference on Advances in visual computing - Volume Part I*, ISVC'11, pages 518–529, Berlin, Heidelberg, 2011. Springer-Verlag. DOI: 10.1007/978-3-642-24028-7_48 18, 20

[34] Bill Buxton. Integrating activity theory for context analysis on large display. In *Human Input to Computer Systems: Theories, Techniques and Technology*, chapter 4. Available online, 2011. DOI: 10.1007/978-3-642-18452-9_7 8

[35] Stuart K. Card, Jock D. Mackinlay, and Ben Shneiderman. Using vision to think. In Stuart K. Card, Jock D. Mackinlay, and Ben Shneiderman, editors, *Readings in Information Visualization*, pages 579–581. Morgan Kaufmann Publishers Inc., San Francisco, CA, 1999. 16

[36] J.M. Carroll, M.B. Rosson, G. Convertino, and C. Ganoe. Awareness and teamwork in computer-supported collaborations. *Interacting with Computers*, pages 21–46, 2006. DOI: 10.1016/j.intcom.2005.05.005 95

[37] Andrew Chetwood, Ka-Wai Kwok, Loi-Wah Sun, George Mylonas, James Clark, Ara Darzi, and Guang-Zhong Yang. Collaborative eye tracking: A potential training tool in laparoscopic surgery. *Surgical Endoscopy*, pages 1–7, 2012. DOI: 10.1007/s00464-011-2143-x 86

[38] George Chin, Jr., Olga A. Kuchar, and Katherine E. Wolf. Exploring the analytical processes of intelligence analysts. In *Proceedings of the 27th international conference on Human factors in computing systems*, CHI '09, pages 11–20, New York, NY, 2009. ACM. DOI: 10.1145/1518701.1518704 78

[39] Adrian Clark, Andreas Dünser, Mark Billinghurst, Thammathip Piumsomboon, and David Altimira. Seamless interaction in space. In *Proceedings of the 23rd Australian Computer-Human Interaction Conference*, OzCHI '11, pages 88–97, New York, NY, 2011. ACM. DOI: 10.1145/2071536.2071549 15

[40] Herbert H. Clark and Susan E Brennan. Grouding in communication. In Lauren B Resnick, John M Levine, and Stephanie Teasley, editors, *Perspectives on Socially Shared Cognition*, pages 127–149. American Psychological Association, 1991. DOI: 10.1037/10096-000 100

[41] William S. Cleveland. *Visualizing Data*. AT&T Bell Laboratories, Murray Hill, NJ, 1993. 3

[42] Diane Cluxton and Stephen Eich. DECIDE hypothesis visualization tool. In *2005 International Conference on Intelligence Analysis*, 2005. 78

[43] UC Berkeley CNMAT. Open sound control. Available at: http://opensoundcontrol.org/introduction-osc. 102

[44] Alistair Cockburn. *Agile Software Development: The Cooperative Game (2nd Edition) (Agile Software Development Series)*. Addison-Wesley Professional, 2006. 98

[45] Andy Cockburn, Amy Karlson, and Benjamin B. Bederson. A review of overview+detail, zooming, and focus+context interfaces. *ACM Comput. Surv.*, 41(1):2:1–2:31, January 2009. DOI: 10.1145/1456650.1456652 36

[46] Dane Coffey, Nicholas Malbraaten, Trung Le, Iman Borazjani, Fotis Sotiropoulos, and Daniel F. Keefe. Slice WIM: A multi-surface, multi-touch interface for overview+detail exploration of volume datasets in virtual reality. In *Proceedings of ACM SIG-GRAPH Symposium on Interactive 3D Graphics and Games*, pages 191–198, 2011. DOI: 10.1145/1944745.1944777 29, 30

[47] Michael Cole. *Cultural psychology*. The Belknap Press of Harvard University Press, Cambridge, MA; London, UK, 2nd edition, 1997. 90, 91

[48] Greg Conti. *Security data visualization: Graphical techniques for network analysis*. No Starch Press, 2007. 97

[49] Armando Cruz, António Correia, Hugo Paredes, Benjamim Fonseca, Leonel Morgado, and Paulo Martins. Towards an overarching classification model of cscw and groupware: a socio-technical perspective. In *Proceedings of the 18th international conference on Collaboration and Technology*, CRIWG'12, pages 41–56, Berlin, Heidelberg, 2012. Springer-Verlag. DOI: 10.1007/978-3-642-33284-5_4 2, 47

[50] Mary Czerwinski, Greg Smith, Tim Regan, Brian Meyers, George Robertson, and Gary Starkweather. Toward characterizing the productivity benefits of very large displays. In *Proceedings of INTERACT 2003*, pages 9–16. IFIP, 2003. 51, 52

[51] Harry Daniels. *Vygotsky and Research*. Routledge, New York, 2008. 90, 91

[52] C. Demiralp and D. Laidlaw. Visweek 2011 panel: Theories of visualization are there any? Available at: http://vis.cs.brown.edu/docs/pdf/Demiralp-2011-TVS.pdf. 77

[53] Leo Denise. Collaboration vs. c-three (cooperation, coordination, and communication). *Innovating*, 7(3), 1999. 1, 47

[54] Anthony DeVincenzi, Lining Yao, Hiroshi Ishii, and Ramesh Raskar. Kinected conference: Augmenting video imaging with calibrated depth and audio. In *Proceedings of the ACM 2011 conference on Computer supported cooperative work*, CSCW '11, pages 621–624, New York, NY, 2011. ACM. DOI: 10.1145/1958824.1958929 15

[55] Paul Dietz and Darren Leigh. Diamondtouch: a multi-user touch technology. In *Proceedings of the 14th annual ACM symposium on User interface software and technology*, UIST '01, pages 219–226, New York, NY, 2001. ACM. DOI: 10.1145/502348.502389 112

[56] Marian Dörk, Sheelagh Carpendale, and Carey Williamson. The information flaneur: A fresh look at information seeking. In *Proceedings of the 2011 annual conference on Human factors in computing systems*, CHI '11, pages 1215–1224, New York, NY, 2011. ACM. DOI: 10.1145/1978942.1979124 27, 76

[57] Marian Dörk, Sheelagh Carpendale, and Carey Williamson. Visualizing explicit and implicit relations of complex information spaces. *Information Visualization*, 11:5–21, 2012. DOI: 10.1177/1473871611425872 28

[58] J Driver. A selective review of selective attention research from the past century. *British Journal of Psychology*, 92(1):53–78, 2001. DOI: 10.1348/000712601162103 82

[59] Colleen M. Duffy. Situation awareness analysis and measurement. *Human Factors and Ergonomics in Manufacturing and Service Industries*, 11(4):383 –384, 2001. 87, 88

[60] Jon Olav Husabø Eikenes. The encyclopedia of human-computer interaction, 2nd ed., 2013. 94

[61] Alex Endert, Christopher Andrews, and Chris North. Professional analysts using a large, high-resolution display. In *IEEE VAST 2009 (Extended Abstract) (Awarded Special Contributions to the VAST Challenge Contest)*, 2009. DOI: 10.1109/VAST.2009.5332485 17

[62] M. R. Endsley. Design and evaluation for situation awarness enhancement. In *Proceedings of the Human Factors Society 32nd Annual Meeting*, pages 97–101. Human Factors and Ergonomics Society, 1998. DOI: 10.1177/154193128803200221 88

[63] Mica R. Endsley and Michelle M. Robertson. Situation awareness in aircraft maintenance teams. *International Journal of Industrial Ergonomics*, 26(2):301–325, 2000. DOI: 10.1016/S0169-8141(99)00073-6 88

[64] Yrjö Engeström. Interactive expertise: Studies in distributed working intelligence. In *University of Helsinki research report*, number Research bulletin 83 in HELDA - The Digital Repository of University of Helsinki, 1992. 2, 47, 48

[65] Yrjö Engeström. *From teams to knots: Activity-theoretical studies of collaboration and learning at work.* Cambridge University Press, Cambridge, UK; New York:, 2008. DOI: 10.1017/CBO9780511619847 91

[66] Danyel Fisher, Rob DeLine, Mary Czerwinski, and Steven Drucker. Interactions with big data analytics. *Interactions*, 19(3):50–59, May 2012. DOI: 10.1145/2168931.2168943 3

[67] M. Freeth, P. Chapman, D. Ropar, and P. Mitchell. Do gaze cues in complex scenes capture and direct the attention of high functioning adolescents with ASD? Evidence from eye-tracking. *Journal of Autism and Developmental Disorders*, 40:534–547, 2010. DOI: 10.1007/s10803-009-0893-2 86

[68] Ben Fry and Casey Reas. Processing. Available at: `http://processing.org/`. 106

[69] Ben Fry, Casey Reas, and John Resig. Processing.js. Available at: `http://processingjs.org/`. 109

[70] ITU GazeGroup. Itu gaze tracker. Available at: `http://www.gazegroup.org/`. 85

[71] Jonathan Grudin. Why CSCW applications fail: Problems in the design and evaluation of organizational interfaces. In *Proceedings of the 1988 ACM conference on Computer-supported cooperative work*, CSCW '88, pages 85–93, New York, NY, 1988. ACM. DOI: 10.1145/62266.62273 69

[72] Jonathan Grudin. Partitioning digital worlds: Focal and peripheral awareness in multiple monitor use. In *Proceedings of the SIGCHI conference on Human factors in computing systems*, CHI '01, pages 458–465, New York, NY, 2001. ACM. DOI: 10.1145/365024.365312 50, 53

[73] Jonathan Grudin and Steven Poltrock. Taxonomy and theory in Computer Supported Cooperative Work. In S. W. Kozlowski, editor, *Handbook of Organizational Psychology*, pages 1323–1348. Oxford University Press, Oxford, UK, 2012. DOI: 10.1093/oxfordhb/9780199928309.001.0001 1, 2, 47, 48, 78

[74] R. Gumienny, L. Gericke, M. Quasthoff, C. Willems, and C. Meinel. Tele-board: Enabling efficient collaboration in digital design spaces. In *Computer Supported Cooperative Work in Design (CSCWD), 2011 15th International Conference on*, pages 47–54, june 2011. DOI: 10.1109/CSCWD.2011.5960054 22, 23

[75] J. Guo and G. Feng. How eye gaze feedback changes parent-child joint attention in shared storybook reading? An eye-tracking intervention study. In *Proceedings in 2011 ACM International Conference on Intelligent User Interfaces (Workshop on Eye Gaze in Intelligent Human Machine Interaction)*, pages 1–8, New York, NY, 2011. ACM. 87

[76] C. Gutwin, S. Greenberg, and M. Roseman. Workspace awareness in real-time distributed groupware: Framework, widgets and evaluation. In *People and Computers XI (HCI'96, London, UK)*, HCI'96, pages 281–298, Swinton, UK, 1996. British Computer Society. DOI: 10.1007/978-1-4471-3588-3_18 57

[77] V. Ha, K.M. Inkpen, R.L. Mandryk, and T. Whalen. Direct intentions: The effects of input devices on collaboration around a tabletop display. In *Horizontal Interactive Human-Computer Systems, 2006. TableTop 2006. First IEEE International Workshop on*, page 8 pp., jan. 2006. DOI: 10.1109/TABLETOP.2006.10 58

[78] Michael Haller, Jakob Leitner, Thomas Seifried, James R. Wallace, Stacey D. Scott, Christoph Richter, Peter Brandl, Adam Gokcezade, and Seth Hunter. The nice discussion room: Integrating paper and digital media to support co-located group meetings. In *Proceedings of the 28th international conference on Human factors in computing systems*, CHI '10, pages 609–618, New York, NY, 2010. ACM. DOI: 10.1145/1753326.1753418 12, 63, 64

[79] Jefferson Y. Han. Low-cost multi-touch sensing through frustrated total internal reflection. In *Proceedings of the 18th annual ACM symposium on User interface software and technology*, UIST '05, pages 115–118, New York, NY, 2005. ACM. DOI: 10.1145/1095034.1095054 8

[80] E. Hetzler and A. Turner. Analysis experiences using information visualization. *Computer Graphics and Applications, IEEE*, 24(5):22–26, Sept.-Oct. 2004. DOI: 10.1109/MCG.2004.22 77

[81] Richards J. Heuer. *Psychology of Intelligence Analysis*. Center for the Study of Intelligence, 1999. 77

[82] James Hollan, Edwin Hutchins, and David Kirsh. Distributed cognition: Toward a new foundation for human-computer interaction research. *ACM Trans. Comput.-Hum. Interact.*, 7:174–196, June 2000. DOI: 10.1145/353485.353487 79

[83] Jim Hollan and Scott Stornetta. Beyond being there. In *Proceedings of the SIGCHI Conference on Human Factors in Computing Systems*, CHI '92, pages 119–125, New York, NY, 1992. ACM. DOI: 10.1145/142750.142769 2

[84] Eva Hornecker. A design theme for tangible interaction: Embodied facilitation. In *Proceedings of the ninth European conference on computer supported cooperative work*, ECSCW'05, pages 23–43, New York, NY, 2005. Springer-Verlag New York, Inc. DOI: 10.1007/1-4020-4023-7_2 13

[85] Eva Hornecker and Jacob Buur. Getting a grip on tangible interaction: A framework on physical space and social interaction. In *Proceedings of the SIGCHI conference on Human factors in computing systems*, CHI '06, pages 437–446, New York, NY, 2006. ACM. DOI: 10.1007/1-4020-4023-7_2 13

[86] Eva Hornecker, Paul Marshall, Nick Sheep Dalton, and Yvonne Rogers. Collaboration and interference: Awareness with mice or touch input. In *Proceedings of the 2008 ACM conference on Computer supported cooperative work*, CSCW '08, pages 167–176, New York, NY, 2008. ACM. DOI: 10.1145/1460563.1460589 58

[87] Elaine M. Huang, Elizabeth D. Mynatt, and Jay P. Trimble. When design just isn't enough: The unanticipated challenges of the real world for large collaborative displays. *Personal Ubiquitous Comput.*, 11(7):537–547, October 2007. DOI: 10.1007/s00779-006-0114-3 68, 69

[88] Jeff Huang, Ryen W. White, and Susan Dumais. No clicks, no problem: Using cursor movements to understand and improve search. In *Proceedings of the 2011 annual conference on Human factors in computing systems*, CHI '11, pages 1225–1234, New York, NY, 2011. ACM. DOI: 10.1145/1978942.1979125 42

[89] Jörn Hurtienne, Christian Stößel, Christine Sturm, Alexander Maus, Matthias Rötting, Patrick Langdon, and John Clarkson. Physical gestures for abstract concepts: Inclusive design with primary metaphors. *Interact. Comput.*, 22:475–484, November 2010. DOI: 10.1016/j.intcom.2010.08.009 39

[90] E. L. Hutchins. How a cockpit remembers its speed. *Cognitive Science*, 19:265–288, 1995. DOI: 10.1207/s15516709cog1903_1 79

[91] Joyent Inc. node.js. Available at: http://nodejs.org/. 111

[92] P. Isenberg, S. Carpendale, A. Bezerianos, N. Henry, and J.-D. Fekete. Coconuttrix: Collaborative retrofitting for information visualization. *Computer Graphics and Applications, IEEE*, 29(5):44 –57, sept.-oct. 2009. DOI: 10.1109/MCG.2009.78 64

[93] P. Isenberg, D. Fisher, M.R. Morris, K. Inkpen, and M. Czerwinski. An exploratory study of co-located collaborative visual analytics around a tabletop display. In *Visual Analytics Science and Technology (VAST), 2010 IEEE Symposium on*, pages 179–186, oct. 2010. DOI: 10.1109/VAST.2010.5652880 23, 48

[94] Petra Isenberg, Niklas Elmqvist, Jean Scholtz, Daniel Cernea, Kwan-Liu Ma, and Hans Hagen. Collaborative Visualization: Definition, Challenges, and Research Agenda. *Information Visualization Journal (IVS)*, 10(4):310–326, 2011. DOI: 10.1177/1473871611412817 16, 17, 18

[95] Petra Isenberg, Danyel Fisher, Sharoda A. Paul, Meredith Ringel Morris, Kori Inkpen, and Mary Czerwinski. Co-located collaborative visual analytics around a tabletop display. *IEEE Transactions on Visualization and Computer Graphics*, 18(5):689–702, may 2012. DOI: 10.1109/TVCG.2011.287 78

[96] Petra Isenberg, Anthony Tang, and Sheelagh Carpendale. An exploratory study of visual information analysis. In *Proceedings of the twenty-sixth annual SIGCHI conference on Human factors in computing systems*, CHI '08, pages 1217–1226, New York, NY, 2008. ACM. DOI: 10.1145/1357054.1357245 78

[97] Don't Click it. Understand it don't click it. Available at: http://dontclick.it. 40

[98] Robert J.K. Jacob, Audrey Girouard, Leanne M. Hirshfield, Michael S. Horn, Orit Shaer, Erin Treacy Solovey, and Jamie Zigelbaum. Reality-based interaction: A framework for post-wimp interfaces. In *Proceedings of the twenty-sixth annual SIGCHI conference on Human factors in computing systems*, CHI '08, pages 201–210, New York, NY, 2008. ACM. DOI: 10.1145/1357054.1357089 7

[99] Jhilmil Jain, Arnold Lund, and Dennis Wixon. The future of natural user interfaces. In *Proceedings of the 2011 annual conference extended abstracts on Human factors in computing systems*, CHI EA '11, pages 211–214, New York, NY, 2011. ACM. DOI: 10.1145/1979742.1979527 7

[100] Ronne Mikkel Jakobsen and Kasper Hornbaek. Sizing up visualizations: Effects of display size in focus+context, overview+detail, and zooming interfaces. In *Proceedings of the 2011 annual conference on Human factors in computing systems*, CHI '11, pages 1451–1460, New York, NY, 2011. ACM. DOI: 10.1145/1978942.1979156 52, 55

[101] Daniel Kahneman. *Thinking, Fast and Slow*. Doubleday Canada, Mississauga, ON, 2011. 73

[102] Martin Kaltenbrunner, Till Bovermann, Ross Bencina, and Enrico Costanza. TUIO - A protocol for table based tangible user interfaces. In *Proceedings of the 6th international workshop on Gesture in human-computer interaction and simulation (GW 2005)*, Vannes, France, 2005. 102

[103] Dietrich Kammer, Jan Wojdziak, Mandy Keck, Rainer Groh, and Severin Taranko. Towards a formalization of multi-touch gestures. In *ACM International Conference on Interactive tabletops and surfaces*, ITS '10, pages 49–58, New York, NY, 2010. ACM. DOI: 10.1145/1936652.1936662 38

[104] Dominik P. Käser, Maneesh Agrawala, and Mark Pauly. Fingerglass: Efficient multiscale interaction on multitouch screens. In *Proceedings of the 2011 annual conference on Human factors in computing systems*, CHI '11, pages 1601–1610, New York, NY, 2011. ACM. DOI: 10.1145/1978942.1979175 36, 37

[105] C. Kelleher and G. Grinstein. The fractal perspective visualization technique for semantic networks. In *Proceedings of the 15th international conference on Information visualisation, IV '11*, pages 211–215, Jul. 2011. DOI: 10.1109/IV.2011.107 24

[106] Azam Khan, Justin Matejka, George Fitzmaurice, Gord Kurtenbach, Nicolas Burtnyk, and Bill Buxton. Toward the digital design studio: Large display explorations. *HumanComputer Interaction*, 24(1-2):9–47, 2009. DOI: 10.1080/07370020902819932 33, 69, 70

[107] KineticJS. Kineticjs - enterprise class web graphics. Available at: http://www.kineticjs.com/. 109

[108] Can Kirmizibayrak, Nadezhda Radeva, Mike Wakid, John Philbeck, John Sibert, and James Hahn. Evaluation of gesture based interfaces for medical volume visualization tasks. In *Proceedings of the 10th international conference on Virtual reality continuum and its applications in industry*, VRCAI '11, pages 69–74, New York, NY, 2011. ACM. DOI: 10.1145/2087756.2087764 25, 27

[109] D. Kirsh. Distributed cognition, coordination and environment design. In *Proceedings of the European Conference on Cognitive Science*, pages 1–10. LEA, 1999. 79

[110] D. Kirsh. Metacognition, distributed cognition and visual design. In P. Gardinfas and P. Johansson, editors, *Cognition, Education and Communication Technology*. Lawrence Erlbaum, 2004. 79

[111] Sungahn Ko, KyungTae Kim, Tejas Kulkarni, and Niklas Elmqvist. Applying mobile device soft keyboards to collaborative multitouch tabletop displays: Design and evaluation. In *Proceedings of the ACM international conference on Interactive tabletops and surfaces*, ITS '11, pages 130–139, New York, NY, 2011. ACM. DOI: 10.1145/2076354.2076379 43, 44

[112] Oleg V. Komogortsev, Dan E. Tamir, Carl J. Mueller, Jose Camou, and Corey Holland. Ema: Automated eye-movement-driven approach for identification of usability issues. In Aaron Marcus, editor, *Design, User Experience, and Usability. Theory, Methods, Tools and Practice - First International Conference, DUXU 2011, Held as Part of HCI International 2011, Orlando, FL, USA, July 9-14, 2011, Proceedings, Part II*, volume 6770 of *Lecture Notes in Computer Science*, pages 459–468. Springer, 2011. 100

[113] Robert Kosara. Info vis 2012 workshop: The role of theory in information visualization. Available at: http://eagereyes.org/blog/2010/infovis-theory-workshop. 77

[114] Robert E. Kraut. Applying social psychological theory to the problems of group work. In *Theories in Human-Computer Interaction*, pages 325–356. Morgan-Kaufmann Publishers, New York, 2002. 48

[115] Zum Kuckuck. Telekom realtime information graphics. Available at: http://projects.zumkuckuck.com/realtime/. 107

[116] Olga Kulyk, Gerrit van der Veer, and Betsy van Dijk. Situational awareness support to enhance teamwork in collaborative environments. In *Proceedings of the 15th European conference on Cognitive ergonomics: The ergonomics of cool interaction*, ECCE '08, pages 5:1–5:5, New York, NY, 2008. ACM. DOI: 10.1145/1473018.1473025 88

[117] K. Kuutti. Activity theory as a potential framework for human-computer interaction research. In B. Nardi, editor, *Context and consciousness: Activity theory and human-computer interaction*, chapter 2, pages 17–44. MIT Press, Cambridge, MA, 1996. 93

[118] Uwe Laufs, Christopher Ruff, and Jan Zibuschka. MT4j - A cross-platform multi-touch development framework. *CoRR*, abs/1012.0467, 2010. 106

[119] Bongshin Lee, Petra Isenberg, Natalie Henry Riche, and Sheelagh Carpendale. Beyond mouse and keyboard: Expanding design considerations for information visualization interactions. In *Information Visualization, 2012. IEEE Symposium on*, 2012. DOI: 10.1109/TVCG.2012.204 27

[120] Bongshin Lee, Petra. Isenberg, Nathalie Henry Riche, and Sheelagh Carpendale. Beyond mouse and keyboard: Expanding design considerations for information visualization interactions. *Transactions on Visualization and Computer Graphics, IEEE*, 18(12):to appear, 2012. DOI: 10.1109/TVCG.2012.204 33, 34

[121] A. N. Leontiev. *Problems of the development of the mind*. MGU, Moscow, 3rd edition, 1972. 90

[122] A. N. Leontiev. *Activity, consciousness and personality*, volume 1978. Prentice Hall, Inc, Englewood Cliffs, NJ, 1978. 90, 91

[123] Kathleen Liston, Martin Fischer, John Kunz, and Ning Dong. Observations of two mep iroom coordination meetings: An investigation of artifact use in aec project meetings. In *CIFE Working Paper #WP106 from Stanford University*, 2007. 66, 67

[124] Jie Liu and Yuanchun Shi. uMeeting: An efficient co-located meeting system on the large-scale tabletop. In Julie Jacko, editor, *Human-Computer Interaction. Users and Applications*, volume 6764 of *Lecture Notes in Computer Science*, pages 368–374. Springer Berlin / Heidelberg, 2011. DOI: 10.1007/978-3-642-21619-0 21, 23

[125] Zimu Liu, Yuan Feng, and Baochun Li. When multi-touch meets streaming. In *Proceedings of the 10th International Conference on Mobile and Ubiquitous Multimedia*, MUM '11, pages 23–32, New York, NY, 2011. ACM. DOI: 10.1145/2107596.2107599 113

[126] Lori Lorigo, Maya Haridasan, Hrönn Brynjarsdóttir, Ling Xia, Thorsten Joachims, Geri Gay, Laura Granka, Fabio Pellacini, and Bing Pan. Eye tracking and online search: Lessons learned and challenges ahead. *J. Am. Soc. Inf. Sci. Technol.*, 59:1041–1052, May 2008. DOI: 10.1002/asi.20794 100

[127] Alessio Malizia and Andrea Bellucci. The artificiality of natural user interfaces. *Commun. ACM*, 55(3):36–38, March 2012. DOI: 10.1145/2093548.2093563 7

[128] N. Marquardt, R. Diaz-Marino, S. Boring, and S. Greenberg. The Proximity toolkit: Prototyping proxemic interactions in ubiquitous computing ecologies. In *ACM Symposium on User Interface Software and Technology - UIST'2011*, page 11 pages, Santa Barbara, CA, October 16-18 2011. ACM Press. DOI: 10.1145/2047196.2047238 112

[129] N. Marquardt, J. Kiemer, and S. Greenberg. What caused that touch? Expressive interaction with a surface through fiduciary-tagged gloves. In *Proceedings of the ACM international conference on Interactive tabletops and surfaces*, ITS '10. ACM Press, 2010. DOI: 10.1145/1936652.1936680 8

[130] Nicolai Marquardt, Ricardo Jota, Saul Greenberg, and Joaquim A. Jorge. The continuous interaction space: Interaction techniques unifying touch and gesture on and above a digital surface. In *Proceedings of the 13th IFIP TC 13 international conference on Human-computer interaction - Volume Part III*, INTERACT'11, pages 461–476, Berlin, Heidelberg, 2011. Springer-Verlag. DOI: 10.1007/978-3-642-23765-2_32 35

[131] Nicolai Marquardt, Johannes Kiemer, David Ledo, Sebastian Boring, and Saul Greenberg. Designing user-, hand-, and handpart-aware tabletop interactions with the touchid toolkit. In *Proceedings of the ACM International Conference on Interactive tabletops and surfaces*, ITS '11, pages 21–30, New York, NY, 2011. ACM. DOI: 10.1145/2076354.2076358 45

[132] Paul W. Mattessich, Marta Murray-Close, and Barbara R. Monsey, editors. *Collaboration: What Makes It Work*. Amherts H. Wilder Foundation, St. Paul, MN, 2001. 47

[133] T. Matthews, T. Rattenbury, and S. Carter. Defining, designing and evaluting peripheral displays: A analysis using activity theory. *Human–Computer Interaction*, 2007. 95

[134] Christopher McAdam and Stephen Brewster. Using mobile phones to interact with tabletop computers. In *Proceedings of the ACM International Conference on Interactive tabletops and surfaces*, ITS '11, pages 232–241, New York, NY, 2011. ACM. DOI: 10.1145/2076354.2076395 35

[135] J. E. McGrath. A typology of tasks. In *Groups: Interaction and Performance*, pages 53–66. Prentice Hall, 1984. 1, 2, 47, 48

[136] K. Moreland. Redirecting research in large-format displays for visualization. In *Large Data Analysis and Visualization (LDAV), 2012 IEEE Symposium on*, pages 91–95. IEEE, 2012. 50

[137] M.R. Morris, A.J.B. Brush, and B.R. Meyers. A field study of knowledge workers' use of interactive horizontal displays. In *Horizontal Interactive Human Computer Systems, 2008. TABLETOP 2008. 3rd IEEE International Workshop on*, pages 105–112, oct. 2008. DOI: 10.1109/TABLETOP.2008.4660192 50, 51

[138] Tomer Moscovich. Contact area interaction with sliding widgets. In *Proceedings of the 22nd annual ACM symposium on User interface software and technology*, UIST '09, pages 13–22, New York, NY, 2009. ACM. DOI: 10.1145/1622176.1622181 42

[139] Patrick Mueller. Web inspector remote. Available at: `http://people.apache.org/~pmuellr/weinre/docs/latest/`. 111

[140] Adiyan Mujibiya, Takashi Miyaki, and Jun Rekimoto. Anywhere touchtyping: Text input on arbitrary surface using depth sensing. In *Adjunct proceedings of the 23nd annual ACM symposium on User interface software and technology*, UIST '10, pages 443–444, New York, NY, 2010. ACM. DOI: 10.1145/1866218.1866262 44

[141] Christian Müller-Tomfelde. *Tabletops - Horizontal Interactive Displays*. Springer Publishing Company, Incorporated, 1st edition, 2010. DOI: 10.1007/978-1-84996-113-4 101

[142] Taichi Murase, Atsunori Moteki, Noriaki Ozawa, Nobuyuki Hara, Takehiro Nakai, and Katsuhito Fujimoto. Gesture keyboard requiring only one camera. In *Proceedings of the 24th annual ACM symposium adjunct on User interface software and technology*, UIST '11 Adjunct, pages 9–10, New York, NY, 2011. ACM. DOI: 10.1145/2046396.2046402 43, 44

[143] B. Nardi, editor. *Context and Consciousness: Activity theory and human-computer interaction*. MIT Press, 1995. 93

[144] Paul Navrtil, Brandt Westing, Gregory Johnson, Ashwini Athalye, Jose Carreno, and Freddy Rojas. A practical guide to large tiled displays. In George Bebis, Richard Boyle, Bahram Parvin, Darko Koracin, Yoshinori Kuno, Junxian Wang, Renato Pajarola, Peter Lindstrom, Andr Hinkenjann, Miguel Encarnao, Cludio Silva, and Daniel Coming, editors, *Advances in Visual Computing*, volume 5876 of *Lecture Notes in Computer Science*, pages 970–981. Springer Berlin / Heidelberg, 2009. 31

[145] Jakob Nielsen. *Usability Engineering*. Morgan Kaufmann Publishers Inc., San Francisco, CA, USA, 1993. 99

[146] Syavash Nobarany, Haraty Mona, and Brian Fisher. Facilitating the reuse process in distributed collaboration: A distributed cognition approach. In *Proceedings of the 2012 ACM conference on Computer supported cooperative work*, CSCW '12, New York, NY, 2012. ACM. DOI: 10.1145/2145204.2145388 79, 80

[147] Nokia. Qt - Cross-platform application and UI framework. Available at: `http://qt.nokia.com/`. 105

[148] Donald A. Norman. Natural user interfaces are not natural. *Interactions*, 17(3):6–10, May 2010. DOI: 10.1145/1744161.1744163 7

[149] NUITeq. Snowflake Suite. Available at: `http://www.nuiteq.com/multitouchsoftware.php`. 105

[150] K. Okada. Collaboration support in the information sharing space. *IPSJ Magazine*, 48(2):123–125, 2007. 1, 47

[151] Gary M. Olson, Thomas W. Malone, and John B. Smith, editors. *Coordination Theory and Collaboration Technology*. Lauwrence Erlbaum Associates, Inc., Mahwah, NJ, 2001. 48

[152] Sami Pietinen, Roman Bednarik, and Markku Tukiainen. Shared visual attention in collaborative programming: A descriptive analysis. In *Proceedings of the 2010 ICSE Workshop on Cooperative and Human Aspects of Software Engineering*, CHASE '10, pages 21–24, New York, NY, 2010. ACM. DOI: 10.1145/1833310.1833314 87

[153] David Pinelle, Carl Gutwin, and Saul Greenberg. Task analysis for groupware usability evaluation: Modeling shared-workspace tasks with the mechanics of collaboration. *ACM Trans. Comput.-Hum. Interact.*, 10(4):281–311, December 2003. DOI: 10.1145/966930.966932 99

[154] David Pinelle, Miguel Nacenta, Carl Gutwin, and Tadeusz Stach. The effects of co-present embodiments on awareness and collaboration in tabletop groupware. In *Proceedings of Graphics interface 2008*, GI '08, pages 1–8, Toronto, Ont., Canada, Canada, 2008. Canadian Information Processing Society. DOI: 10.1145/1375714.1375716 59

[155] Catherine Plaisant, Brett Milash, Anne Rose, Seth Widoff, and Ben Shneiderman. Life-lines: visualizing personal histories. In *Proceedings of the SIGCHI Conference on Human Factors in Computing Systems*, CHI '96, pages 221–227, New York, NY, USA, 1996. ACM. DOI: 10.1145/238386.238493 74

[156] Christopher Plaue and John Stasko. Presence & placement: Exploring the benefits of multiple shared displays on an intellective sensemaking task. In *Proceedings of the ACM 2009 international conference on Supporting group work*, GROUP '09, pages 179–188, New York, NY, 2009. ACM. DOI: 10.1145/1531674.1531701 8, 65, 80

[157] Marshall Scott Poole, David R. Seibold, and Robert D. McPhee. Group decision-making as a structurational process. *Quarterly Journal of Speech*, 71(1):74, 1985. DOI: 10.1080/00335638509383719 48

[158] M. I. Posner and M. K. Rothbart. Research on attention networks as a model for the integration of psychological science. *Annu Rev Psychol*, 58:1–23, 2007. DOI: 10.1146/annurev.psych.58.110405.085516 83, 84

[159] Dmitry Pyryeskin, Mark Hancock, and Jesse Hoey. Extending interactions into hover-space using reflected light. In *Proceedings of the ACM International Conference on Interactive tabletops and surfaces*, ITS '11, pages 262–263, New York, NY, 2011. ACM. DOI: 10.1145/2076354.2076406 42

[160] Arne Raeithel and Boris M. Velichkovsky. Joint attention and co-construction: New was to foster user-designer collaboartion. In B. Nardi, editor, *Context and Consciousness: Activity Theory and Human-Computer Interaction*, chapter 9, pages 199–233. MIT Press, Cambridge, MA, 1996. 93

[161] Carl Ratner. *Vygotsky's sociohistorical psychology and its contemporary applications*. Plenum Press, New York, NY, 1991. DOI: 10.1007/978-1-4899-2614-2 90

[162] C. Reas and B. Fry. *Getting Started with Processing*. Make Series. O'Reilly Media, 2010. 107

[163] Jennifer M. Riley, Mica R. Endsley, Cheryl A. Bolstad, and Haydee M. Cuevas. Collaborative planning and situation awareness in army command and control. *Ergonomics*, 49(12-13):1139–1153, 2006. DOI: 10.1080/00140130600612614 57, 58

[164] G. Robertson, M. Czerwinski, P. Baudisch, B. Meyers, D. Robbins, G. Smith, and D. Tan. The large-display user experience. *Computer Graphics and Applications, IEEE*, 25(4):44–51, july-aug. 2005. DOI: 10.1109/MCG.2005.88 51, 52

[165] Y. Rogers. Distributed cognition and communication. In Keith Brown, editor, *Encyclopedia of Language & Linguistics*, pages 731–733. Elsevier, Oxford, 2nd ed. edition, 2006. 79

[166] Yvonne Rogers and Sin Lindley. Collaborating around vertical and horizontal large interactive displays: Which way is best? *Interacting with Computers*, 16(6):1133–1152, 2004. DOI: 10.1016/j.intcom.2004.07.008 65

[167] Yvonne Rogers, Helen Sharp, and Jenny Preece. *Interaction Design: Beyond Human - Computer Interaction*. Wiley Publishing, 3rd edition, 2011. 98

[168] Jaime Ruiz, Yang Li, and Edward Lank. User-defined motion gestures for mobile interaction. In *Proceedings of the 2011 annual conference on Human factors in computing systems*, CHI '11, pages 197–206, New York, NY, 2011. ACM. DOI: 10.1145/1978942.1979341 39

[169] J. Salerno, D. Hinman, and D. Boulware. Building a framework for situation awareness. In *Proceedings of the 7th International Conference on Information Fusion*, 2004. 89, 90

[170] Dominik Schmidt, Ming Ki Chong, and Hans Gellersen. Handsdown: Hand-contour-based user identification for interactive surfaces. In *Proceedings of the 6th Nordic conference on human-computer interaction: Extending boundaries*, NordiCHI '10, pages 432–441, New York, NY, 2010. ACM. DOI: 10.1145/1868914.1868964 45

[171] Dominik Schmidt, Ming Ki Chong, and Hans Gellersen. Idlenses: Dynamic personal areas on shared surfaces. In *ACM International Conference on Interactive tabletops and surfaces*, ITS '10, pages 131–134, New York, NY, 2010. ACM. DOI: 10.1145/1936652.1936678 36, 45

[172] Sebastian Schmidt, Miguel A. Nacenta, Raimund Dachselt, and Sheelagh Carpendale. A set of multi-touch graph interaction techniques. In *ACM International Conference on Interactive tabletops and surfaces*, ITS '10, pages 113–116, New York, NY, 2010. ACM. DOI: 10.1145/1936652.1936673 36

[173] Nicolas Schneider, Peter Bex, Erhardt Barth, and Michael Dorr. An open-source low-cost eye-tracking system for portable real-time and offline tracking. In *Proceedings of the 1st Conference on Novel gaze-controlled applications*, NGCA '11, pages 8:1–8:4, New York, NY, 2011. ACM. DOI: 10.1145/1983302.1983310 85

[174] S. D. Scott, A. Allavena, K. Cerar, G. Franck, M. Hazen, T. Shuter, and C. Colliver. Investigating tabletop interfaces to support collaborative decision-making in maritime operations. In *Proceedings of International Command and Control Research and Technology Symposium*, 2010. 71, 72

[175] S. D. Scott, F. Sasangohar, and M. L. Cummings. Investigating supervisor-level activity awareness displays for command and control operations. In *Proceedings of HSIS 2009: Human Systems Integration Symposium*, 2009. 71

[176] S. D. Scott, J. Wan, A. Rico, C. Furusho, and M.L. Cummings. Aiding team supervision in command and control operations with large-screen displays. In *Proceedings of HSIS 2007: ASNE human systems integration symposium*, 2007. 71

[177] Stacey D. Scott and Antoine Allavena. Investigation of a prototype naval planning tool for tabletop computing research. In *Report prepared for Defence Research and Development Canada - Atlanta*, number CSL2010-01 in Collaborative Systems Laboratory, pages 1–38, 2010. 71, 72

[178] Stacey D. Scott, Antoine Allavena, Katie Cerar, Phillip McClelland, and Victor Cheung. Designing and assessing a multi-user tabletop interface to support collaborative decision-making involving dynamic geospatial data. In *Report prepared for Defence Research and Development Canada - Atlanta*, number CSL2010-02 in Collaborative Systems Laboratory, pages 1–11, 2010. 71

[179] Stacey D. Scott, Karen D. Grant, and Regan L. Mandryk. System guidelines for co-located, collaborative work on a tabletop display. In *Proceedings of the eighth European conference on computer supported cooperative work*, ECSCW'03, pages 159–178, Norwell, MA, 2003. Kluwer Academic Publishers. 33

[180] Orit Shaer and Eva Hornecker. Tangible user interfaces: Past, present, and future directions. *Found. Trends Hum.-Comput. Interact.*, 3(1–2):1–137, January 2010. DOI: 10.1561/1100000026 13

[181] B. Shneiderman. The eyes have it: A task by data type taxonomy for information visualizations. In *Visual Languages, 1996. Proceedings., IEEE Symposium on*, pages 336–343, sep 1996. DOI: 10.1109/VL.1996.545307 74

[182] Ben Shneiderman. Tree visualization with tree-maps: 2-d space-filling approach. *ACM Trans. Graph.*, 11(1):92–99, January 1992. DOI: 10.1145/102377.115768 74

[183] Garth Shoemaker, Takayuki Tsukitani, Yoshifumi Kitamura, and Kellogg S. Booth. Whole body large wall display interfaces. In *Proceedings of the 28th of the international conference extended abstracts on Human factors in computing systems*, CHI EA '10, pages 4809–4812, New York, NY, 2010. ACM. DOI: 10.1145/1753846.1754236 35

[184] Terri Simmons. What's the optimum computer display size? *Ergonomics in Design*, 9(19):19–27, 2001. DOI: 10.1177/106480460100900405 52

[185] David Canfield Smith, Charles Irby, Ralph Kimball, and Eric Harslem. The star user interface: An overview. In *Proceedings of the June 7-10, 1982, national computer conference*, AFIPS '82, pages 515–528, New York, NY, 1982. ACM. DOI: 10.1145/1500774.1500840 101

[186] Peng Song, Wooi Boon Goh, Chi-Wing Fu, Qiang Meng, and Pheng-Ann Heng. Wysi-wyf: exploring and annotating volume data with a tangible handheld device. In *Proceedings of the 2011 annual conference on Human factors in computing systems*, CHI '11, pages 1333–1342, New York, NY, 2011. ACM. DOI: 10.1145/1978942.1979140 29, 30

[187] Martin Spindler, Marcel Martsch, and Raimund Dachselt. Going beyond the surface: studying multi-layer interaction above the tabletop. In *Proceedings of the 2012 ACM annual conference on Human Factors in Computing Systems*, CHI '12, pages 1277–1286, New York, NY, 2012. ACM. DOI: 10.1145/2207676.2208583 13, 27

[188] Martin Spindler, Christian Tominski, Michel Hauschild, Heidrun Schumann, and Raimund Dachselt. Novel fields of application for tangible displays above the tabletop. In *ACM International Conference on Interactive tabletops and surfaces*, ITS '10, pages 315–315, New York, NY, 2010. ACM. DOI: 10.1145/1936652.1936743 26, 27

[189] Martin Spindler, Christian Tominski, Heidrun Schumann, and Raimund Dachselt. Tangible views for information visualization. In *ACM International Conference on Interactive tabletops and surfaces*, ITS '10, pages 157–166, New York, NY, 2010. ACM. DOI: 10.1145/1936652.1936684 27

[190] Susan G. Straus and Joseph E. McGrath. Does the medium matter? The interaction of task type and technology on group performance and member reactions. *Journal of Applied Psychology*, 79(1):87–97, 1994. DOI: 10.1037/0021-9010.79.1.87 1, 2, 47, 48

[191] Lucy Suchman. *Plans and situated action: The problem of human-machine communication*. Cambridge University Press, 4th edition, 1994. 96

[192] Diseree Sy. Adapting usability investigations for agile user-centered design. *Journal of Usability Studies*, 2(3):112–132, May 2007. 98, 99

[193] Desney S. Tan, Darren Gergle, Peter G. Scupelli, and Randy Pausch. Physically large displays improve path integration in 3d virtual navigation tasks. In *Proceedings of the SIGCHI conference on Human factors in computing systems*, CHI '04, pages 439–446, New York, NY, 2004. ACM. DOI: 10.1145/985692.985748 53

[194] Desney S. Tan, Jeanine K. Stefanucci, Dennis R. Proffitt, and Randy Pausch. The info-cockpit: Providing location and place to aid human memory. In *Proceedings of Predominantly Undergraduate Institutions*, PUI '01, pages 1–4, New York, NY, 2001. 52

[195] James J. Thomas and Kristin A. Cook. *Illuminating the Path: The Research and Development Agenda for Visual Analytics*. National Visualization and Analytics Ctr, 2005. 16, 77

[196] Alice Thudt, Uta Hinrichs, and Sheelagh Carpendale. The Bohemian bookshelf: Supporting serendipitous book discoveries through information visualization. In *Proceedings of*

the 2012 ACM annual conference on Human Factors in Computing Systems, CHI '12, pages 1461–1470, New York, NY, 2012. ACM. DOI: 10.1145/2207676.2208607 76

[197] M. Tobiasz, P. Isenberg, and S. Carpendale. Lark: Coordinating co-located collaboration with information visualization. *Visualization and Computer Graphics, IEEE Transactions on*, 15(6):1065–1072, nov.-dec. 2009. DOI: 10.1109/TVCG.2009.162 24, 25

[198] Tobii. Tobii technology. Available at: http://www.tobii.com/. 85

[199] M. Tomasello. Human culture in evolutionary perspective. *Advances in culture and psychology*, pages 1–48, 2010. DOI: 10.1093/acprof:oso/9780195380392.003.0001 81

[200] Jay Trimble, Wales Roxana, and Ric Gossweiler. Nasa's merboard: An interactive collaborative workspace platform. In *Nasa Techdocs*, number 20040010824 in Nasa techdocs, pages 1–27, 2003. 67

[201] Greg Trubulenz. Touchable. Available at: https://github.com/dotmaster/Touchable-jQuery-Plugin. 109

[202] Philip Tuddenham, Ian Davies, and Peter Robinson. Websurface: An interface for co-located collaborative information gathering. In *Proceedings of the ACM International Conference on Interactive tabletops and surfaces*, ITS '09, pages 181–188, New York, NY, 2009. ACM. DOI: 10.1145/1731903.1731938 24, 25

[203] Philip Tuddenham and Peter Robinson. Territorial coordination and workspace awareness in remote tabletop collaboration. In *Proceedings of the 27th international conference on Human factors in computing systems*, CHI '09, pages 2139–2148, New York, NY, 2009. ACM. DOI: 10.1145/1518701.1519026 59

[204] Edward R. Tufte. *Envisioning Information*. Graphics Press, Cheshire,CT, 1990. 3

[205] Edward R. Tufte. *Visual Explanations: Images and Quantities, Evidence and Narrative*. Graphics Press, Cheshire,CT, 1997. 3

[206] Edward R. Tufte. *Beautiful Evidence*. Graphics Press, Cheshire,CT, 2006. 3

[207] J. W. Tukey. *Exploratory data analysis*. Addison-Wesley, Boston, MA, 1977. 3

[208] Christophe Viau. Scripting inkscape with d3.js. Available at: http://christopheviau.com/d3_tutorial/d3_inkscape/. 111

[209] Stephen Voida and Elizabeth D. Mynatt. It feels better than filing: Everyday work experiences in an activity-based computing system. In *Proceedings of ACM CHI 2009 Conference on Human Factors in Computing Systems*, CHI '09, pages 259–268, New York, NY, 2009. ACM. DOI: 10.1145/1518701.1518744 94

[210] Stephen Voida, Elizabeth D. Mynatt, and W. Keith Edwards. Re-framing the desktop interface around the activities of knowledge work. In *Proceedings of the 21st annual ACM symposium on User interface software and technology*, UIST '08, pages 211–220, New York, NY, USA, 2008. ACM. DOI: 10.1145/1449715.1449751 94

[211] Stephen Voida, Matthew Tobiasz, Julie Stromer, Petra Isenberg, and Sheelagh Carpendale. Getting practical with interactive tabletop displays: designing for dense data, "fat fingers," diverse interactions, and face-to-face collaboration. In *Proceedings of the ACM International Conference on Interactive tabletops and surfaces*, ITS '09, pages 109–116, New York, NY, 2009. ACM. DOI: 10.1145/1731903.1731926 35, 36

[212] Ulrich von Zadow. libavg. Available at: `http://https://www.libavg.de/site/`. 106

[213] Ulrich von Zadow, Florian Daiber, Johannes Schöning, and Antonio Krüger. Globaldata: multi-user interaction with geographic information systems on interactive surfaces. In *ACM International Conference on Interactive tabletops and surfaces*, ITS '10, pages 318–318, New York, NY, 2010. ACM. DOI: 10.1145/1936652.1936746 106

[214] L. S. Vygotsky. *Mind in Society*. Harvard University Press, Cambridge, MA; London, 1978. 90

[215] L. S. Vygotsky. *Thought and Language*. MIT Press, Cambridge, MA, 1986. 90

[216] L.S. Vygotsky. The methods of reflexological and psychological investigation. In Rene van der Veer and Jann Valsiner, editors, *The Vygotsky Reader*, pages 27–45. Wiley, 1994. 90

[217] James Wallace. *The impact of shared and personal devices on collaborative process and performance*. PhD thesis, University of Waterloo, Canada, 2012. 65

[218] James R. Wallace, Stacey D. Scott, Eugene Lai, and Deon Jajalla. Investigating the role of a large, shared display in multi-display environments. *Computer Supported Cooperative Work*, 20:529–561, 2011. DOI: 10.1007/s10606-011-9149-8 61

[219] James R. Wallace, Stacey D. Scott, Taryn Stutz, Tricia Enns, and Kori Inkpen. Investigating teamwork and taskwork in single- and multi-display groupware systems. *Personal and Ubiquitous Computing*, 13:569–581, 2009. DOI: 10.1007/s00779-009-0241-8 60, 61

[220] James V. Wertsch. *Vygotsky and the Social Formation of Mind*. Harvard University Press, Cambridge MA; London, 1985. 90

[221] James V. Wertsch. *Mind as Action*. Oxford University Press, New York, 1998. 91

[222] Daniel Wigdor, Hao Jiang, Clifton Forlines, Michelle Borkin, and Chia Shen. WeSpace: The design development and deployment of a walk-up and share multi-surface visual collaboration system. In *Proceedings of the 27th international conference on Human factors in computing systems*, CHI '09, pages 1237–1246, New York, NY, 2009. ACM. DOI: 10.1145/1518701.1518886 28, 29

[223] Daniel Wigdor and Dennis Wixon. *Brave NUI World: Designing natural user interfaces for touch and gesture.* Morgan Kaufmann Publishers, San Francisco, CA, 1st edition, 2011. 4, 7, 34, 93

[224] A. Pike William, John Stasko, Remco Chang, and Theresa A. O'Connell. The science of interaction. *Information Visualization*, 8(4):263–274, 2009. DOI: 10.1057/ivs.2009.22 75

[225] Andrew D. Wilson. Using a depth camera as a touch sensor. In *ACM International Conference on Interactive tabletops and surfaces*, ITS '10, pages 69–72, New York, NY, 2010. ACM. DOI: 10.1145/1936652.1936665 42

[226] Jacob O. Wobbrock, Meredith Ringel Morris, and Andrew D. Wilson. User-defined gestures for surface computing. In *Proceedings of the 27th international conference on Human factors in computing systems*, CHI '09, pages 1083–1092, New York, NY, 2009. ACM. DOI: 10.1145/1518701.1518866 37, 38, 39

[227] J.M. Wolfe. Visual search. *Attention*, 1:13–73, 1998. 83

[228] Pak Chung Wong and J. Thomas. Visual analytics. *IEEE Computer Graphics and Applications*, 24(5):20 – 21, sept.-oct. 2004. DOI: 10.1109/MCG.2004.39 16, 77

[229] T. Wypych, S. Yamaoka, K. Ponto, and F. Kuester. System for inspection of large high-resolution radiography datasets. In *Aerospace Conference, 2011 IEEE*, pages 1–9, march 2011. DOI: 10.1109/AERO.2011.5747534 18, 20

[230] Xiaoxin Yin, William Yurcik, Michael Treaster, Yifan Li, and Kiran Lakkaraju. Visflowconnect: Netflow visualizations of link relationships for security situational awareness. In *Proceedings of the 2004 ACM workshop on Visualization and data mining for computer security*, VizSEC/DMSEC '04, pages 26–34, New York, NY, 2004. ACM. DOI: 10.1145/1029208.1029214 90, 91

[231] B. Yost and C. North. The perceptual scalability of visualization. *Visualization and Computer Graphics, IEEE Transactions on*, 12(5):837–844, sept.-oct. 2006. DOI: 10.1109/TVCG.2006.184 54

[232] Beth Yost, Yonca Haciahmetoglu, and Chris North. Beyond visual acuity: The perceptual scalability of information visualizations for large displays. In *Proceedings of the SIGCHI conference on Human factors in computing systems*, CHI '07, pages 101–110, New York, NY, 2007. ACM. DOI: 10.1145/1240624.1240639 50, 54, 55

[233] Fang You, HuiMin Luo, and JianMin Wang. Integrating activity theory for context analysis on large display. In Zhigeng Pan, Adrian David Cheok, Wolfgang Müller, and Xubo Yang, editors, *"Transactions on edutainment V"*, pages 90–103. Springer-Verlag, Berlin, Heidelberg, 2011. 93

[234] Nicola Yuill and Yvonne Rogers. Mechanisms for collaboration: A design and evaluation framework for multi-user interfaces. *Transactions of Human–Computer Interaction (TOCHI)*, 2012. DOI: 10.1145/2147783.2147784 5, 7, 81, 82

[235] William Yurcik. Tool update: Visflowconnect-IP with advanced filtering from usability testing. In *Proceedings of the 3rd international workshop on Visualization for computer security*, VizSEC '06, pages 63–64, New York, NY, 2006. ACM. DOI: 10.1145/1179576.1179588 90, 91

Authors' Biographies

ROBERT BIDDLE

Robert Biddle is a Professor at Carleton University, appointed to the School of Computer Science and the Institute of Cognitive Science. His research interests are in Human-Computer Interaction, and his current work is on usable computer security and on surface technologies for collaborative work. He leads themes for two Governement of Canada NSERC Strategic Research Networks, ISSNet (Internetworked Systems Security) and SurfNet (Surface Applications), and leads the project on Usable Privacy and Security for GRAND, the Industry Canada Network of Centers of Excellence. He has over 200 refereed research publications, and university awards for teaching and research.

JUDITH BROWN

Judith Brown is a post doctoral fellow at Carleton University working in Prof. Biddle's Human-Oriented Technology Software Lab. She received her Ph.D. in Psychology, specializing in Human-Computer Interaction, by conducting field studies of collaborative software teams. She is currently engaged in a project for creating team room software enabling large surfaces for use by Agile software teams. She also works on a project to enable collaborative analysis work of incidents in data centers. She was a professor in Computer Science and Software Engineering for 15 years and has many publications in software engineering and HCI. She has 6 years of experience as a developer in the telecommunications field.

STEVENSON GOSSAGE

Stevenson Gossage is a graduate student working on designing collaborative software for team rooms. He is designing and developing a multitouch agile cardwall to help with the ongoing planning work of software projects. He is particularly interested in the design of natural gestures, and is developing a gesture set for interaction with the cardwall. He leverages theories of situation awareness and shared team awareness in his work. The design of the cardwall is also being based on guidelines for shared awareness. As a result, the cardwall application will support a transparent planning process for software teams, inspire conversation, and encourage communication.

CHRIS HACK

Chris Hack is a graduate student working on leveraging visual attention in human-computer interactions, especially in collaborative situations in which knowledge of where others are visually attending can improve collaboration. He is also developing a low cost, head-mounted, eye-tracker which has the potential to be used with any display surface. Having worked in industry for several years on web-development projects, Chris is an experienced software engineer. When he is not working on his research he is a teaching assistant for undergraduate computer science students on subjects that include software usability and software engineering.

JEFF WILSON

Jeff Wilson is a graduate student in Computer Science. He has over fifteen years of industry experience with computers, working his way from field technician to developer team lead before shifting to focus on research in Human Computer Interaction. His past development experience includes workflow automation, business data migration, call center reporting, electronic document management, and creation of proprietary development and deployment frameworks and tools. His current interests are interaction design methodology and development of mixed-presence collaboration tools for surface technologies.

Printed in the United States
by Baker & Taylor Publisher Services